PLACE OF NO RETURN

Place *of* No Return

HOW I SURVIVED CHINA'S UYGHUR CAMPS

Mihrigul Tursun
Andrea C. Hoffmann

ENGLISH EDITION TRANSLATED BY
Rachel Hildebrandt Reynolds

TITLETOWN
PUBLISHING

TitleTown Publishing LLC
Green Bay, Wisconsin USA

TitleTown Publishing, LLC
P.O. Box 12093 Green Bay, WI 54307-12093
920.737.8051 | titletownpublishing.com
Publisher: Tracy C. Ertl
Editor: Lori A. Preuss

PUBLISHER'S CATALOGING-IN-PUBLICATION DATA
(Provided by Cassidy Cataloguing Services, Inc.).

Names: Tursun, Mihrigul, 1989- author. | Hoffmann, Andrea Claudia, author. |
Reynolds, Rachel Hildebrandt, translator.

Title: Place of no return : how I survived China's Uyghur camps / Mihrigul Tursun,
Andrea C. Hoffmann ; English edition translated by Rachel Hildebrandt Reynolds.

Other titles: Ort ohne Wiederkehr. English.

Description: English edition. | Green Bay, WI : TitleTown Publishing, LLC, [2023]
| English translation of: Ort ohne Wiederkehr : wie ich als Uigurin Chinas Lager
überlebte (München : Wilhelm Heyne Verlag, 2022).

Identifiers: ISBN: 9781955047210

Subjects: LCSH: Tursun, Mihrigul, 1989- | Women genocide survivors--Biography. |
Detention of persons-- China--Personal narratives. | Uighur (Turkic people)--China--
Xinjiang Uygyr Zizhiqu--Biography. | Uighur (Turkic people)--China--Xinjiang Uygyr
Zizhiqu--Social conditions. | Uighur (Turkic people)--Persecutions--China--Xinjiang
Uygyr Zizhiqu. | Internment camps-- China--Personal narratives. | Hostages--Abuse
of--China--Xinjiang Uygyr Zizhiqu. | Involuntary sterilization-- China--Xinjiang
Uygyr Zizhiqu. | Ethnic conflict--China--Xinjiang Uygyr Zizhiqu. | Xinjiang Uygyr
Zizhiqu (China)--Ethnic relations. | China--Ethnic relations. | Ethnic conflict--China.
| Human rights--China. | Political persecution--China. | Persecution--China. | Uighur
diaspora. | LCGFT: Autobiographies. | BISAC: BIOGRAPHY & AUTOBIOGRAPHY
/ Survival. | RELIGION / Religious Intolerance, Persecution & Conflict.

Classification: LCC: DS731.U4 T8713 2023 | DDC: 305.8/943230516092--dc23

TABLE OF CONTENTS

PROLOGUE

After a long flight, our plane landed in Washington. Due to the time difference between Egypt and the United States, the sun was still shining when we arrived. Having slept for the last third of the trip, my children stretched and gazed curiously out the window.

"We're here," I told them. "This is our new home!"

"So many planes," my three-year-old declared in amazement. He could hardly wait to get off our plane and out on the tarmac. I fished our bags out of the overhead bins and corralled him and his twin sister toward the exit. As we reached the gangway, the afternoon sun shone on our faces.

An Arab passenger helped us to snag a cart for our luggage. We then found ourselves standing in line at the security checkpoint as I tightly clutched the hands of my two little ones on each side. I could hardly believe that we had made it to American soil. But when the immigration officers appeared, I felt my children grow fidgety and reluctant to continue walking. With eyes wide, they stared at the men in uniform and their dogs as they snuffled among the baggage, searching for drugs.

"They're going to beat us!" my son cried out, terrified.

Suddenly, both children yanked their hands out of mine and dashed away. I set off after them, abandoning our luggage where it stood. I trailed the two runaways, who had already vanished into the crowd of people. I disregarded every barrier tape I encountered and caused a flurry of commotion in my wake. The security officers were immediately alarmed.

"Hey, you have to stand in line!" one of them barked at me.

At that very moment, I discovered my children hiding under a table. I hurried over to them, but they were trembling in fear because they could see that one of the security officers was on my heels.

"They're going to arrest you! Run away, Mama!" my daughter warned me.

"What's going on here?" the uniformed officer asked loudly.

"My children are scared of you," I explained to him.

"I can see that, but why?" Although the man was over six feet tall and carrying a gun, he seemed clueless about why anyone might be frightened of him.

The Arab woman who had helped us with our bags walked up at that moment. She asked the officer if he minded lowering his voice. And she pulled out some candy, which she held out to the children, who were still cowering fearfully under the table.

They slowly calmed back down. "You are such smart children," I told them when, after a little coaxing, they were willing to slowly walk back, hand in hand, to the border control checkpoint. "But you don't need to be scared anymore. We're in America now; we're safe."

Nonetheless, I could understand their panic-stricken reaction. The three of us had been through a lot. We had just escaped hell itself.

CHAPTER 1

An Uyghur in China

I come from Toraklik, a village not far from Qarqan, an oasis town in the Taklamakan Desert in the farthest western reaches of China. This place has nothing in common with the high-tech China that the world of today knows. At least back at the time of my birth in 1989, time seemed to stand still in my homeland.

I was born in a donkey cart. The vehicle was supposed to carry my mother from our village to Korla, the closest larger town with a hospital. Usually, the women in our region give birth to their children at home. However, I started my arrival into the world too early and was also in a dangerous lateral position. This was why my mother needed a doctor to help with the delivery. The long, bumpy cart ride was the only way to reach him. However, she didn't make it; my parents were only halfway there when I came. There were severe complications during the delivery, and my mother, who was only seventeen years old at the time, did not survive my birth.

My father, Tursun, was inconsolable. He had married my mother only one year before. They were very much in love and had dreamed of having a large family. But suddenly, all that remained was anguish and a tiny baby who bawled for her mother's milk.

In accordance with Islamic rite, my mother was buried that very same day. After that, the family council gathered to decide what should be done with me. Nobody thought that my odds of survival were all that good. I was almost six weeks premature and much too small. So tiny, in fact, that I was told I could fit into my father's hat. This was why everyone thought I would die. Only my old grandmother, my mother's mother, who had just lost her daughter, clung to the hope that at least her granddaughter might live.

She made my father an offer. "Give the little one to me. I will try to get some weight on her."

My grandmother was in deep mourning like everyone else, but perhaps she felt that if she were fortunate enough to keep me alive, it would help her cope with losing her beloved daughter. My grandmother always saw a part of my mother in me: the part that was still alive. This was why she wanted to take care of the little creature in whose veins flowed the blood of her daughter Malika.

In addition, my grandmother immediately understood that my father would be completely overwhelmed by the demands of raising a newborn all on his own. She, on the other hand, knew a lot about children. After all, she had brought 24 of them into the world and raised them.

My mother had been her youngest child, but my grandmother had another daughter who had yet to marry. My Aunt Menzire strongly resembled my mother; just like my grandmother and me, she was a small, very delicate woman. Compared to the people from our region, her skin tone was light, and her facial features were soft. In addition, she possessed the same dark brown, slightly wavy hair that practically reached her hips, and she was only a year and a half older than my mother. Thus, my grandmother was almost sure that my father would also like her. She suggested that he marry Menzire after an appropriate mourning period. After considering this briefly, my father agreed to establish a new family with Menzire.

All this explains why I grew up in my grandmother's home. She lived in a modest plaster building a short distance from Toraklik, while my father and aunt lived in a different village. We visited them once a month, or the two of them came to our house to see me. As a result, I have always had a very close relationship with them and consider Menzire a kind of surrogate mother. However, the primary and most important caregiver in my life was my grandmother, a woman who had already reached old age by the time I was born but who was full of warmth and kindness.

Early on, she had a very difficult time with me since I was quite sick after my early and tragic birth. For a while, nobody knew if I could survive without my mother's milk, but my grandmother owned a cow and four sheep. And she was patient. Whenever I demanded to be fed, she dunked her finger into a bowl of sheep's milk and let me suck on it as if it were my mother's breast. This way, she managed to put some meat on my bones through significant effort on her part; I grew stronger and gained weight as time passed. When I was finally over the worst, and it was clear that I would live, my grandmother allowed herself to rejoice in her twenty-fifth child without reservation. She proudly and confidently told everyone that Allah had been especially good to her.

In many ways, my grandmother represented a world that no longer exists today. That world was already in the process of disappearing during my childhood, but we were unaware of that. Over 4,000 kilometers away from Beijing, we lived in a kind of parallel universe. Even our clocks ran differently since the sun rose much later here than in the Chinese heartland. I was not even aware in my earliest years that I lived in a country called China. Whenever we spoke about our homeland, my relatives always called it East

Turkestan. This was why I naturally believed this was our country's name.

In my mind, the Chinese were foreigners with narrow eyes, flat noses, and no body hair. Chinese women never bound their hair into braids, and the men did not wear beards or head coverings, as did the people who lived in our village. We, children, were warned to watch out for the Chinese and when in doubt, to run away from them since they liked to eat Uyghur children. I believed that – we all believed that – which was why we were so glad that no Chinese people ever showed up in our village.

In material terms, we lived modestly. Some would have said in impoverished conditions. I did not find it that way at the time, but when I look back now and compare our standard of living to those in other regions of China, I can recognize it. My grandmother's house had neither electricity nor running water. To replenish our drinking water, she sent me every day with two buckets to a nearby lake, which supplied water to the oasis.

My chores included tending the animals. After the morning milking, I would lead our sheep and the cow to a few places where enough grass and greenery grew for them to eat their fill during the day. At the same time, I had to make sure that the animals did not run away. Later, when I went to school, I had to search for spots along my way where I could tie them up and leave them until I could fetch them again after school.

Whenever I determined that one of our animals was pregnant, my grandmother's wrinkled face would beam with joy. We were always glad when the lambs came because they brought us additional milk, wool, and meat. One time, a sheep even gave birth to twins. My grandmother considered what we could do with this boon.

"We could sell it and buy ourselves some warm clothes – or we could keep it and stuff our jackets with the wool," she told me. In the winter, we always needed especially warm clothing.

However, Grandmother had not included the mother sheep in her plans. The latter had no desire to nurse two lambs simultaneously, so she would only allow the larger lamb to nurse and reject the smaller, weaker one. It would sit in the corner and wail, bawling for food. I was horrified by such cruelty. My grandmother tried in vain to reconcile the mother and her younger offspring but eventually gave up.

"She won't accept it," she declared after countless attempts.

"But we can't just let it die!"

"No." Grandmother instructed me to hunt for a special bottle in the shed. It had a suction device on the top and looked like a baby bottle. She filled it with some of the milk that remained from the milking. "We will have to raise it ourselves," Grandmother said. "This is now your responsibility."

And so, I suddenly found myself in the role of mother sheep: I gave the little lamb its bottle several times a day, and it always took it hungrily and impatiently. After a few days, it grew stronger and its coat fluffier. It even eventually began to examine its environment beyond the sheep pen. I was very happy with my efforts.

The sheep were our livelihood and played a major role in our diet. We butchered one of them every year in conjunction with a special occasion. We stored the meat in a pit underneath our house since we did not own a refrigerator. Of course, we also cooked a lot of the meat right after the butchering to share it with our neighbors and relatives in the village. This was our tradition: every day, a different village family cooked and shared food with all the neighbors. This way, there was usually something warm to eat, even if someone had no food in storage or did not wish to cook.

We ate whatever came up in the small garden behind our house. My grandmother cultivated beets, beans, potatoes, tomatoes, and other vegetables. There were also fruit trees with delectable apricots and pomegranates that tasted unbelievably sweet once they were ripe. I was known to stuff my stomach full of them, and my grandmother would fuss at me. "You should give the other children some of them," she would scold, as sharing food was very important in our culture.

Although my grandmother and I lived independently, somewhat outside the village, we often had company since many of my aunts and uncles lived nearby. They dropped by regularly, and my numerous cousins around my age also paid us visits.

My best friend was Khoshgul, our neighbor's delicate, sickly daughter. I loved to play "family" with her. When we played this game, the two of us pretended to be mothers taking care of our doll children, but of course, we did not have any actual dolls. We had no store-bought toys, only the things we made ourselves. Our dolls were large carrots into which we carved faces with a knife. The green tops were our carrot children's hair. We cradled them in our arms, fed them, and put them to bed like real children – or even like real dolls.

Occasionally Khoshgul or other children would spend the night at our house. We would all sleep in my grandmother's large bed. She woke us up early in the morning because as soon as the first rooster crowed, it was time for the morning prayer. My grandmother would don a veil, kneel on the floor, and recite the set Arab prayers. We, the children, were supposed to repeat after her and imitate the movements of her prayer. Instead, I often played little jokes on her. For example, when she touched her head to the ground, I slipped up next to her unnoticed and poked her in the side. My grandmother was quite ticklish. At first, she would try to ignore me, but eventually, she could not help it. She would break into peals of laughter in the middle of the prayer. We, the children, would double over as well.

The Islamic faith was a natural part of our day-to-day lives. Grandmother and I wore our best clothes every Friday and went to the mosque. The entire village gathered there for Friday prayers.

It was a matter of seeing and being seen, and there was always someone there who handed out sweets to us children, usually almonds or raisins. I quickly stuck these treasures in my pockets and savored them slowly throughout the week. Until the following Friday, when we gathered again, these delicacies would be replenished.

I also enjoyed the fasting month of Ramadan. My grandmother, however, was very strict and insisted that we could not even have tea or water during the day. Depending on whether Ramadan fell in the warm or the cold time of year, this could be very hard. But my grandmother was convinced we needed to strengthen our willpower and learn to resist temptation. "This is true freedom," she would impress upon me. And as a reward for the day's deprivations, we would eat big evening meals among relatives.

Although she raised me piously like this, we did not practice an especially intensive or extreme form of Islam. None of our relatives did that. On the contrary, my father placed great value on the fact that we Uyghurs were more liberal when it came to religious matters than the Arabs. For example, Uyghur women only rarely wore head coverings. What was much more common was for men to wear them. And we girls went around unveiled and wore our hair bound into lots of little braids.

During the first years of my life, I spoke only Uyghur with my grandmother, neighbors, and relatives. The lessons at the village school were also only given in Uyghur. This had much to do with Deng Xiaoping, who took over as leader of the Community Party after Mao Zedong; he granted our region relatively extensive autonomy during the 1980s. However, this era was already ending during my school days in the 1990s. By this point, Beijing was trying to gain increasing control over us once more, piece by piece.

The directional change was probably evident in other parts of the Xinjiang province earlier. However, in my remote village, we did not hear about this for a long time. I did not see any ethnic

PLACE OF NO RETURN

Chinese people with my own eyes until I was ten years old when a Chinese man and woman unexpectedly appeared in our schoolyard. I recognized them because they looked just like the descriptions we had read about them, at least with respect to their noses. They also had short hair.

My classmates, curious, surrounded them. Khoshgul and I also approached the strangers cautiously. My friend was slower than I was.

"Do you think they're as dangerous as the adults say?" she whispered to me.

"Are you scared they'll eat you?" I teased her.

"You're crazy!"

The Chinese pair revealed themselves to be quite friendly. They chatted with several students and wanted to know which of us could speak Chinese. The woman also had scissors with her. She offered each of us girls a ten yuan reward if we let her cut off one of our braids. Ten yuan! That was an astronomical sum to me; I had never held that much money. Whenever Grandmother sent me into the village for soap or flour, she never gave me more than half of that amount. In my head, I calculated what I could buy with that much money. And besides, what was just one braid? I had nineteen of them on my head. So one more or less would not make any difference. "Come on, we'll do it as a dare," I goaded Khoshgul.

She gazed at me out of her white face and incredibly wide eyes. "You're going to let them cut off one of your braids?"

"What's the big deal? Don't you have the guts to do it?" I provoked her further. I mainly wanted to shore up my spirits by saying this. Khoshgul, however, was not impressed. She shook her head disapprovingly.

"What about you, girl? Do you want the prize?" the Chinese woman asked me directly. She had been watching us, and I nodded shyly.

"Well, then come here." she urged me.

8

I was already standing inside the circle and was the focus of my classmates' attention. There was no turning back now without losing face. "What's your name?" the woman asked.

"Mihrigul."

"That is a pretty name. And how many braids do you want me to cut today, Mihrigul?"

"Two," I heard myself say.

"Two," she repeated, and I thought I heard admiration in her voice. "Did you hear that, children? Your classmate is a very brave girl!"

While still speaking, the woman took her long scissors and stepped closer to my hair. I heard a snip – and one of my dark braids plummeted to the ground. I felt dizzy, but the second snip was already following. The woman smiled. "Here you go, brave girl," she said as she handed me two ten-yuan notes. The face of the perennially youthful-looking Chairman Mao smiled up at me.

Back at home with my grandmother, the entire experience struck me as absurd. I tried to turn my head so she could not see that the braids were missing. The woman had unfortunately taken ones that were not low at the back of my neck but from a rather conspicuous spot up close to my face.

Grandmother stared at me with eagle eyes. "Who did this to you?" she demanded of me. I admitted that two Chinese people had shown up at that school.

"Did they force you to do it?"

"No." Grandmother's face revealed she was upset, so I could not tell her about the money I had received. "Other students let them cut their braids, too," I pointed out.

This information, however, only seemed to make her more furious. "Didn't I tell you you can never trust the Chinese?"

"But they were nice…," I declared defensively.

"Nice," she hissed at me. "They disfigured you! What Uyghur

man will be interested in a girl who simply gives away her beautiful braids?"

I stared at Grandmother with huge eyes. I had never given any thought to men until now, but I swore high and low that I would never again let someone cut my long hair.

Starting in the fifth grade, all the students in my school had to learn Chinese. We even received a Chinese teacher, Mr. Hu, a gaunt man with glasses. He drilled us on the Chinese characters. At first, they were completely foreign to us because the written Uyghur uses the Arabic alphabet. Now everything was inverted: every word was represented by a single, sometimes quite complicated logogram.

In the evenings, I would sit with my grandmother at the table and practice drawing the characters to memorize them better. She was very interested in my studies since she had never gone to school herself; she was illiterate. However, by explaining the meaning of each character, I was able to help her make up a little for that. She also listened enthusiastically to my Chinese vocabulary words. When I demonstrated how Mr. Hu enunciated the words, the two of us often dissolved into laughter. Chinese sounds so different from Uyghur, and the words are also completely different. My grandmother tried to memorize a few of them, but she was not very successful. "It doesn't matter," I consoled her. "That's why you have me."

"Yes," she replied thoughtfully. "It doesn't make much difference to me anymore, but you must study diligently. These characters are the gateway to the world. They can give you wings that will carry you far beyond our village."

I did not understand what she meant, but I tried hard. After all, I wanted my grandmother to be proud of me.

One year after we started our Chinese lessons, the school principal announced that all students had to take an exam. After I informed my grandmother about this, she gave me no peace. She even temporarily released me from all my chores, so I could use every minute to study.

"Do your best, my little flower." My nickname was a play on the meaning of my name, which translates as "gentle flower." "Show them what you're made of," she whispered in my ear the morning of the test.

I think that was some magic spell; at least, it had a magical effect. I sensed that the moment I started the first exercise, which was incredibly easy. Throughout the day, it felt like my grandmother stood behind me, showing me the correct answers to the questions. The Chinese characters appeared in my mind's eye – and all I had to do was brush them onto the paper in front of me.

Two weeks later, the principal called me to his office. I was a little worried and wondered if I had done something wrong. I knocked on his office door a little apprehensively. "Come in!" he called from inside.

I opened the door. There sat the principal and my Chinese teacher, Mr. Hu. "Don't just stand there! Come in," he urged cheerfully in Chinese.

"Congratulations!" the principal declared after I stepped inside the room. My principal was also suddenly speaking Chinese now. I glanced in confusion from one man to the other. What did this all mean?

"You made the best test score in the school," the principal announced, pointing at a pile of papers on his desk. "You did a great job. How old are you, Mirighul?"

"Twelve," I replied.

"And you live with your grandmother?"

I nodded timidly.

"She will be very happy to hear this news," he said. "You have won a scholarship! After the summer break, you will be allowed to attend a different school, a boarding school in Guangzhou. This is a great honor. Are you glad? Of course, you can come home during the school breaks."

I felt simultaneously hot and cold. Yes, Grandmother would surely be happy, I thought. But this meant that I would have to live somewhere else, right? "Where is Guangzhou?" I asked.

My home village and the city of Guangzhou were separated by no less than 4,000 kilometers. My trip to the South China coast took five days and five nights. I first went by bus to Korla, where I met the other children from Xinjiang who had been chosen for the program. We covered the rest of the distance on the train, accompanied by a teacher.

I cannot say that I was happy. I naturally felt proud that I had received the best test score in our school, but I was unsure what to think of the scholarship prize. My grandmother also seemed to feel torn on the matter. On the one hand, all the hopes she had pinned on me were now fulfilled. "This is a huge opportunity for you, my child," she emphasized repeatedly. "Now you can achieve great things in life." On the other hand, the scholarship meant that our paths had to diverge – and she was just as sad about that as I was, if not more so. At least secretly.

In the weeks before my departure, we both attempted to conceal the pain that this parting was causing us. I silently wondered several times if I could decline the scholarship or let someone else take it. However, this idea seemed so outlandish that no one ever mentioned it to me as a possibility, neither the principal nor my grandmother. It was just a given that a student would do whatever the school administration declared.

My grandmother just spent the entire time before I left talking about how important it was for me to study hard and to get a good job someday. "I want you to have a career and to be a rich woman," she urged. "You won't live in this village and milk sheep anymore."

She was quite taken with this thought, and because I loved her so much and wanted to see her happy, I made her wish my own. "Then I'll buy you a nice coat, and we'll go to Mecca together," I promised her.

However, on the day of my departure, we could no longer keep up the charade. We both stood at the bus stop and bawled. "Don't forget to call your father so he can keep me informed about your progress," she reminded me because she did not own a phone. And then the bus drew up. I had to board and leave her behind. It broke my heart as I waved at her through the window and watched her grow smaller and smaller.

On this trip, I realized for the first time how huge the country was in which I lived. First, we crossed the Taklamakan Desert with its imposing dunes, followed by the snow-covered mountain range surrounding it. We then drove to Ürümqi, the modern provincial capital with skyscrapers and multi-lane roads. However, I experienced my greatest surprise when we left Xinjiang. The landscape suddenly became much greener than I had ever known it to be back home. The rails led to the huge metropolises of Gansu, Xian, and Wuhan until we finally reached the coast on the fifth day.

We had reached our destination. I suddenly found myself in China when I stepped down from the train. I had spent my entire life in China, but until this point, it had never felt like that. In Xinjiang, the Chinese had always seemed like outsiders to us. But now, there were only Chinese as far as I could see, and they stared at me as if I were an outsider. That was very unsettling for me.

Guangzhou is a gigantic city, and everything about it was unfamiliar to me: the air tasted damp and like exhaust fumes; the climate was warmer; the people hurried down the streets, talking a blue streak into their small phones; cars clattered everywhere. It felt as if I had landed on the moon. What annoyed me more than anything was that everyone around me suddenly spoke Chinese. After all, the fact that I earned the highest score on the test at my village school did not mean that I knew the language well. On the contrary, I only understood a small fraction of the words people directed at me in the early days after my arrival.

Wide-eyed, I trotted after the teacher, who led me to my new school, a large, modern building. My dorm room was located on the ninth floor, and I shared it with five other girls, all of whom were ethnic Chinese and came from different parts of the country. They chatted with each other as we made our beds. I was the only one who remained silent because I could not express myself yet. With difficulty, I tried to figure out what they were talking about, but whenever they asked me a question, all I could do was shrug. This frustrated me greatly; robbed of my language, I felt inferior. The other Uyghurs I met in the schoolyard, and the cafeteria probably felt similarly. However, the teachers intervened whenever we tried to talk to each other. They told us we had to try to speak only Chinese here. This was why only one Uyghur was allowed to live in each dorm room.

At first, it was extremely difficult for me to adjust to my new life. I was painfully homesick for my village. I missed my old classmates, Khoshgul from next door, my sheep, the clear and dry desert air, the chilly nights in Xinjiang, and my aunt's steamed noodles. But above all, I missed my grandmother; what I would have given for her to wake me up just once more and compel me to say morning prayers with her! Or to dig around in the vegetable garden with her. I would have even gladly mucked out the sheep pen with her in those moments.

My father had given me a used cell phone, but I could not do anything with it because I had no credit for it. However, I was glad when he called every other week. "Are things going well at school? Are you studying hard?" he always asked during our short chats.

"Yes," I lied. I felt incapable of telling him I still had no friends and could understand nothing in my classes.

"Your grandmother also sends her love," he said occasionally. My heart leaped at those times, but I was also worried. My scholarship was only guaranteed for one year, and its extension would depend on my grades. At the time, I could hardly imagine that they would end up especially high. What would Grandmother say if I returned after one year and had to tell her that I had not used my opportunity in the way she had wanted me to? She would be quite disappointed in me if that happened. "You should have tried harder." I could already hear her reproach in my ears.

My fear of letting her down inspired me to start studying with fervor. I was determined to learn as many characters as it took to understand the Chinese textbooks and follow my lessons. And so I memorized and practiced the characters in every free moment. Even after the other girls had fallen asleep, I lay stretched out under my sheet with a flashlight, working on the characters. This was pretty much the only time I had all to myself. Our days were otherwise strictly regimented with classes, joint mealtimes, and athletic activities like soccer and volleyball.

My language skills improved over time. I noticed that it grew easier to follow my classmates' conversations and grasp their gist. And the words my teachers uttered no longer sounded as incomprehensible as they had at the beginning. Nonetheless, I still felt quite lonely. This might have been because I concentrated too much on my Chinese studies or being a little shy by nature. In any case, it was hard for me to make friends with Chinese girls.

In my isolation, I turned more intensely to religion. I had not taken Islam all that seriously in my old life because it had been a natural, though not dominant, part of our days. But suddenly, my faith was very important to me. I think it was because this was one final link between me and my homeland. My religion distinguished me from the other girls, so I refused to give it up under any circumstances. Like my grandmother, I now insisted on keeping the prayer times, at least the morning ones.

While the other girls were still asleep, I would climb out of bed, pull on a shawl, and mumble the set prayers my grandmother had recited to me. I also executed the series of movements as she did. It helped me feel closer to her; I knew she would have been pleased if she could have seen me. After the ritual part of the prayer, I also added a freeform in which I conversed with God. I talked to Him as if He were a good friend with whom I could chat about my day and share my secrets. I also told Him what was worrying me, what I wished for, and what I had done that I was ashamed of. All of this had a remarkably calming effect on me. After one of these conversations, I felt fortified for the day. It seemed as if I were under the protection of a higher power – and that I could not veer far off my course as long as He held His hand over me.

"What are you doing?" Yangjali asked me one day when she woke up just as I was bowing toward Mecca. She was the girl who slept in the bed below mine. Whenever I climbed down the ladder past her, I often saw her blink at me. She probably thought I was heading to the bathroom and then fell asleep. However, she watched me today and wanted to discuss it.

"I was praying," I replied truthfully. She stared at me, baffled. She had no idea what I meant by that. Or perhaps she thought we were having a language problem. "I was talking to God," I explained more specifically, hoping that my actions would be clearer as a result.

But her face looked more confused than ever now. "With God?" she repeated. "What is that? What do you mean?"

I now started to feel uncertain about whether I had correctly expressed myself. I knew the characters for "God" and "prayer," but should I have pronounced them differently? We needed to get ready for class by this point, so there was no time to discuss the matter further. However, I made a mental note to look up the words in my dictionary again because I wanted to give Yangjali a satisfactory answer.

That evening, after supper, we resumed our conversation. I drew the characters for her on a piece of paper to make sure she understood what I meant. She laughed. "You believe in a God?" she asked, amused.

I was perplexed. "Yes, of course. Don't you?"

"No. That's a very old, unscientific concept."

We studied each other like two creatures from different stars.

There was real curiosity between us. Yangjali wanted to know what was going on with my "God," and I was curious about what she believed in if not in Him. "Who do you think created the Earth and humans?" I prompted her.

"Well, the Earth was created in the Big Bang – and humans evolved from apes."

"You can't honestly believe that!" She did not bat an eyelash; obviously, she was being serious.

"Well, I believe that God created me."

"There is no God!"

"Of course, there's a God!" I shot back.

"How do you know that?"

"I talk to Him every single morning."

"And? Does he answer back?"

"Of course!" I waxed poetic about how my God led and protected me. Yangjali and the other girls listened attentively. "I can tell Him about anything that's bothering me," I said. "He shows me which way I should go."

"My parents do that for me," our roommate Wanchauwa interjected.

"Yes, but God's much better!" I argued.

"Why?"

"Well, because He's just always there! Even if you don't have any money to make a phone call, you can talk to Him just like that."

Wanchauwa nodded, this advantage making sense to her.

"And even if I've done something wrong, I can tell Him about it and ask for forgiveness."

I had piqued my classmates' curiosity. After this conversation, Yangjali and Wanchauwa kept coming and asking me to tell them more about my God and the Islamic faith. At first, I thought they just wanted to make fun of me, but then I realized their interest was sincere, so I told them everything I knew. They also got books for themselves, and when we started to work with computers at the school, they researched things online. At this point, they noticed differences between how I lived and the rules of Islam.

"But you don't pray five times a day!" Wanchauwa confronted me at one point.

"Yes, but I do at least once a day," I defended myself.

"And you don't wear a headscarf!"

"Women don't necessarily have to wear a headscarf. In my village, only a few of them do." I explained to her that these rules were not all carved in stone and that you could adapt them to your circumstances.

"Can you show me how you pray?" she asked.

I never intended to convert anyone to Islam, but Yangjali and Wanchauwa refused to let things go. Maybe they were yearning for spirituality because we lived in a boarding school environment. Whatever the case, they eventually wanted to know what they had to do to become Muslims. I felt overwhelmed and wished that there had been a cleric nearby. However, we were not in a position to search for a mosque since we were never allowed to leave the school campus. And so we researched online how someone could convert to Islam – and were successful in our search. "It says here that you have to adopt an Islamic name and say the Shahada in the presence of a Muslim," I read aloud.

"The Shahada?"

"Yes, the Islamic creed."

I knew our creed, of course – and could even say it in Arabic. After all, I had heard the statement in the mosque every Friday. And so I recited it for them: "*La ilaha illa Allah wa Muhammad rasul Allah* – There is no God except Allah, and Muhammad is his messenger."

The two Chinese girls solemnly repeated it after me. They then gazed at me expectantly. "We still need new names," Wanchauwa reminded me, wanting to do everything by the book as always. And so we decided that Wanchauwa would henceforth be called Muriman and Yangjali would go by Aischa.

"Well, that's it," I said. "You're now Muslims!"

They looked a little skeptical, but then their faces broke into smiles. "Really?" they asked happily.

"Yes, really," I assured them. "Congratulations!"

Yangjali and Wanchauwa became my best friends. We shared a dorm room during my five years at the boarding school. We always called each other by our Islamic names, and I went by Mina. And thus, we created a secret world beyond the boundaries of our school lives. However, my sisters in faith adhered to the Islamic rules more strictly than I did.

Both of them immediately stopped eating pork and started wearing headscarves. They criticized me for not doing the same, but it was fine for them to talk. They were Han Chinese, which meant that they were under no restrictions regarding their religion. Therefore, they could believe what they wanted. However, this was not the case for me. As an Uyghur, the teachers expected me to assimilate as much as possible. And since I was quite ambitious, I did not want to jeopardize my academic career. I could always hear my grandmother's words in my head: "You can achieve anything. Just work hard!"

And that was what I did; I was a very diligent student. My Chinese was soon on par with that of native speakers, and every year, before our final exams, I studied so hard that my head pounded and my eyes burned. These exams were very important for me. Only those students who did very well on the tests received extensions to their scholarships for the following year. This was why I was under enormous pressure to do well. I had no desire to return to my village and to have to admit to my grandmother that I was no longer allowed to continue my studies. I would have never forgiven myself for that.

However, even with the scholarship, making ends meet in Guangzhou was not easy for me. My tuition and lodging at the school were covered, but every student had to pay for their own food and clothes. Almost all the students received money from their parents for that. My father also sent me money every month, but it was never close to enough because life here was so much more expensive than it was in Xinjiang. Even if I had only ordered the cheapest meal possible in the school cafeteria, I would have had nothing left over for notebooks or shampoo.

I knew my father was sending me as much money as possible, so I never asked for more. I had to find another solution, so I asked the school cafeteria manager if he needed help in the kitchen. He gazed at me with sympathetic eyes. "But you have to do your schoolwork. When could you work here?" he asked.

"On the weekends!"

We did not have any lessons on Saturdays and Sundays. Some students used that time to visit their families, but that was not possible for me. This was why the manager eventually relented and allowed me to wash dishes in the cafeteria on the weekends. I was very pleased to get this opportunity to earn a little extra money. If I spent my money wisely, I could perhaps even save enough to purchase a coat for my grandmother at graduation, like I had promised when I left home.

The kitchen job did not remain my only one. The longer I lived in Guangzhou, the better my jobs got. I helped out with the large Canton Fair and worked as a translator for an import-export business. Eventually, I earned a decent amount for a student, and with my income, I could finally buy a smartphone. This simplified my communication with my family back home since I could call my father several times a week after that.

He was a good conversationalist. We had not spent much time together during my childhood, but I had always felt like he cared for me and supported me as best he could. He also encouraged me to invest a lot in my education. "Very few people receive a chance as you have. Use it wisely," he often said. And I almost believed I could hear my grandmother's voice in his.

I still missed my grandmother greatly. Whenever I asked about her, he said that she was doing well. However, I could never speak with her because her house still had no electricity or phone. It was awful; I had not been able to speak with her for years. How was she doing? I could hardly wait to go home after my last exam and hug her.

After five years, I graduated with honors. I also won a university scholarship. Proud of my accomplishments, I bought a ticket to fly back to Ürümqi and another for the next leg to Korla. Back at school, I bid my friends goodbye. "Are you glad to be going back home?" Muriman asked.

I could not even find the words to express how happy I was.

The flight took eight hours. It was a ridiculously short time compared to the five days and nights I spent on the train ride to the school. Nonetheless, the hours felt like an eternity. I finally caught sight of the barren, dry landscape of my home province below me. The majestic mountains glistened whitely, and my heart pounded faster. I had missed all this so much!

My father and Aunt Minzire were waiting for me at the airport. I saw them from afar and hurried toward them. However, with a touch of disappointment, I registered that my grandmother had not come with them. But, of course, I told myself she was an old woman and should avoid unnecessary exertions.

I kissed my parents and let my half-brother pick up my suitcase. With amazement, I realized that he was already a teenager. "I'm so glad to be back with all of you," I declared as we walked toward the car my father had borrowed from a neighbor, especially for the occasion. But only one desire burned in my heart. "Are we driving straight to Grandmother's?"

My father stared at the ground, then slowly shook his head. "Please forgive me. I should have told you long before now, but I thought it would upset you and interfere with your studies …."

"What happened?" I asked nervously.

"Your grandmother is no longer alive," he said with a gulp. "She died over two years ago."

CHAPTER 2

Wedding with Obstacles

The flight attendant made one more pass down the aisle, urging the passengers to turn off their electronic devices and fasten their seatbelts. With an acquiescent smile, the man sitting beside me ended his call and switched his phone to airplane mode. We then started to taxi toward the runway, and the plane took off.

I took a deep breath. It was a good feeling to be up in the air. The plane was carrying me to Cairo, where I wished to study. After my grandmother's death, there hadn't been much to keep me in my home village. First, I returned to Guangzhou and earned my bachelor's degree in business administration. I subsequently worked for an import-export company for a while, but I wanted to get my master's degree abroad. London was my first choice; however, it was too expensive, and I couldn't find any scholarships. I was eventually admitted to a university in Cairo. This was a good compromise for me since I calculated that the money I had saved, combined with my grandmother's small inheritance and the amount my father could contribute, would be just enough to cover my expenses for exactly one year. I had learned a little Arabic in school, and besides that, the language sounded familiar to me because we had always recited the prayers out of the Koran.

"Are you flying all by yourself to Egypt?" my seatmate inquired.

I studied him; he was elegantly dressed and had light brown eyes that were edged with long eyelashes. His facial features told me that he was Arab, although he was speaking in English.

"Yes, I'll be studying at the British University in Cairo," I replied in his native language. I didn't know much Arabic, but the man was thrilled.

"Are you? Your language skills are amazing," he claimed.

Of course, it wasn't true, but I thought it was nice of him to say that. He told me that, until recently, he had also been a student at the same university where I was about to begin. I could hardly believe it!

"Really?"

"Yes, really. What a coincidence!"

The man introduced himself as Mahmud. As the flight attendant distributed coffee and cookies, I asked him about Cairo and my new university. He described it to me in glowing colors and praised the international environment that dominated the campus.

"Many students, like you, come from other countries because its reputation is so good."

"And the professors?"

"Most of them come from Egypt or other Arab countries. That's why it's good that you've already learned a little Arabic."

"I'll be taking a language course parallel to my academic classes."

He thought this was a good idea. Mahmoud assured me that the level of research and teaching at the British University was quite high.

"British standards dominate everything," he declared. And once you have a diploma from there in your pocket, the world will be your oyster. It is recognized everywhere."

I was naturally delighted to hear this. I had hoped this was the case because I was far from convinced that I wanted to return to my province, or even to China, after finishing my degree. Perhaps I would become an international businesswoman or at least set off in that direction. Mahmoud was also a businessman. He told me that he regularly flew to Guangzhou to purchase goods for his clothing shop in Cairo.

"The clothes made in China are cheaper than those in Turkey," he explained, "and the quality is comparable. Maybe you'd like to stop by sometime and tell me if you agree."

"I certainly will."

We chatted throughout the entire flight. When we landed ten hours later, I didn't feel exhausted; I felt downright exhilarated. Mahmud accompanied me by taxi to the inn where I stayed that night. He encouraged me to contact him if I ever needed anything.

"Just call me," he said. "It doesn't matter what for."

We became friends. In those early days, Mahmud helped me find my place in my new world. He showed me around the city and explained to me how everything worked.

I initially lived in a dormitory where many other Chinese and Uyghur students lived. However, I didn't feel at home there. It wasn't particularly clean, and the rent struck me as overpriced. Mahmoud helped me to find an apartment off campus, which I shared with two friends. Aja was an Arab student in my department; Tanja had roots in Barcelona and worked as an au pair. I got along quite well with both of them.

Our life together reminded me of my time in boarding school, although my current existence involved more freedom and self-determination. Nobody told me how to schedule my days, what to eat or wear, or when to go to bed. There were also fewer rules that pertained to my studies than had been the case in China. I was finally able to pick out the subjects that truly interested me. I was my own master!

In terms of religion, I also felt freer; in Egypt, nobody ever looked suspicious if you identified yourself as Muslim. After all, almost everyone here was Muslim. I found this quite comfortable. I occasionally visited the world-famous al-Azhar Mosque on Fridays with some Uyghur friends because renowned clerics always preach there. But, of course, we didn't want to miss out on that. And we always bound headscarves around our stylishly bleached hair before entering the mosque.

Everything was going well. Even my Arabic skills improved markedly, so I was quite hopeful that I could complete my studies without a hitch. I had no idea that anything could thwart my plans, and I could already see myself holding my diploma from the university, but then that all came apart.

Political unrest spread throughout Egypt. The Arab Spring had begun, and after the dictator, Ben Ali, was deposed in Tunisia, the people of Cairo also took to the streets to demonstrate against their long-time president Hosni Mubarak. Young people my age, in particular, were no longer willing to accept misgovernance, the state's arbitrary willfulness, and the numerous repressive measures the regime exercised over its people. Instead, they demanded better living conditions, freedom, and social justice.

I found this quite interesting. People gathering in public squares to express their discontent was a new concept to me. I had never experienced anything like this in China. But did we Chinese perhaps also have enough reasons to stage protests? Perhaps in my home province, where the Chinese treated us Uyghurs like children and imposed their will on us, we did. I banished the thought. After all, I wasn't in China but in Egypt. Should I protest along with the others? No, I decided. This wasn't my government, nor was it my fight. Nonetheless, I rejoiced with the Egyptians when they managed to topple their tyrant after only four weeks of demonstrations.

I celebrated with Mahmoud; we were overjoyed. That wasn't the case for the Chinese government. The revolutionary events in Egypt made the rulers in Beijing nervous. They were probably afraid that the insubordination against the Cairo rulers might also infect us. In any case, the Chinese government ordered all students to return home from the Arab nations. The Communist Party made an official statement about being concerned for our safety, but I'm certain there was something else behind it. Specifically, the strong religious component to the Arab revolution and the strengthening of the Muslim Brotherhood shortly after that must have made the powers-that-be in Beijing uncomfortable.

I was disappointed when I received the summons by email to return home immediately. Studying abroad had always been my great dream, and since I didn't come from a wealthy or influential family, realizing this dream had cost me an incredible amount of effort and stress. And now "they" wanted to take that success away from me.

"I don't want to go back," I admitted to my friends one evening as we gathered to dine on a lentil and rice dish Aja had prepared. "I've invested too much into this degree."

"I understand," my Arab friend replied. "But what can you do? You can't just ignore the request, can you?"

"Well…" I said thoughtfully.

This was the pivotal question. What would happen if I disregarded the summons and remained in Egypt? Initially, nothing. However, my visa would expire within a few months, and no extension would be granted. I wouldn't be allowed to stay in Egypt past that point. And once I returned to China, I would doubtlessly face all sorts of trouble. No, that didn't sound like a particularly smart course of action. My courage sank.

"So, the Chinese students are supposed to return," Aja declared. "But what about the Chinese citizens who live here permanently?"

"They have a different status."

"Then that is what you need to get."

"And how am I supposed to do that?"

"Couldn't you marry an Egyptian?"

I stared at her in disbelief momentarily, but then her suggestion worked through my brain. After closer consideration, what sounded so outlandish at first hearing might be a realistic possibility. As the wife of an Egyptian man, I would have to be allowed to stay in the country, especially since, in Egypt's patriarchal society, wives were considered a kind of property of their husbands. "But who could I marry at such short notice?" I wondered out loud.

My friends exchanged meaningful glances, then broke out in peels of laughter. "Why, it's obvious: Mahmud, of course!" Tanja said as Aja nodded energetically.

"Mahmud?" I had no idea how they had landed at this absurd idea. They had certainly realized that Mahmud and I were friends; there was no way they could have missed that. However, that didn't mean I could ask him to marry me. I blushed as I thought of this. "But we're just friends...." I added.

"So what?" Tanja asked, ever practically minded. "That doesn't matter. You'd just be married on paper only. The main point is that you could then stay here legally."

"Just ask him! I'm sure he'd do it," Aja also encouraged me.

But I firmly rejected this option. I would have preferred to ask a perfect stranger to marry me than to trouble my best friend with this. What would Mahmud think of me? That I had fallen in love with him? Or even worse: that I was willing to exploit his good nature?

Aja pensively stroked the abaya she put on whenever she left our apartment, which was now lying on the chair next to her. She murmured something about how we foreigners were more straitlaced than she ever would have thought we could be. "How about I put out a few feelers for you?" she grinned.

To my great astonishment, Mahmud agreed to the plan. He didn't even have to think about it for very long. "Of course, let's get married!" he exclaimed the next time we met close to campus in a student cafe. "I already told you I'd always be there for you."

I blushed with embarrassment. "That is very kind of you," I squeezed out, unable to say more.

"What are you talking about? It would be a great honor to marry you."

And so Mahmud and I spent the next few months planning our wedding. Even if we only aimed for a marriage of convenience, thorough preparations needed to be made. The authorities required a stunning amount of paperwork and documents from us. We both had to produce our birth certificates and school transcripts. In addition, I had to procure an officially notarized certificate from China verifying that I was considered unmarried there.

Naturally, this presented a problem. According to the regulations, my father had to confirm that I was still unmarried. There was no way around it. So I had to ask him to draw up this document for me, and he was instantly suspicious.

"Why do you need this?" he asked when I made this request on the phone.

"For the university," I lied. "You have no idea how complicated it is here. Without this, they won't extend my student permit." If considered objectively, this wasn't really a lie since I truly wouldn't have been able to continue my studies without doing this.

"Well, I'll look into it," my father said, only slightly mollified.

"It is incredibly important," I prodded him so he would take the matter seriously. "Listen, my studies and career depend on this certificate!"

When we finally had all the papers in hand, we thought we could get an appointment at the registry office. But then we ran into the small matter of the witnesses, which according to Egyptian law, were required for the marriage. No marriage ceremony, not even a civil one like ours, could occur without the families being present. In my case, things were simpler; we argued that my family lived in China and couldn't travel to Egypt for the wedding. But for Mahmud, we had a harder time finding an excuse. We concocted all sorts of tall tales. We claimed that his siblings had all emigrated, and his parents were too old and weak to participate in a wedding. None of this was true. We hadn't informed anyone about our plans to get married since this was just a marriage of convenience. In the end, we convinced the authorities, and instead of our families, five registry office employees served as our witnesses.

Now that this hurdle was finally cleared, we could focus on the enjoyable part of our project: the question of what we would wear. I insisted on being married in white. "The registry people shouldn't have any suspicions," I argued to Mahmud.

In reality, I was slowly starting to get excited. Whether this was a marriage of convenience or not, this would be my wedding! It was a significant day in my life–and I wanted to dress and prepare myself properly.

Mahmud agreed with me completely. "Yes, I want to see you in a long, white dress. I'm sure you'll look stunning in it, Mihrigul," he said.

Mahmud even offered to cover the cost of my wedding gown. I told him that he was crazy. Why should he go to the expense? After all, he was doing all of this as a favor to me. Nonetheless, he insisted, and so I set off with my friend Aja to try on dresses. After our classes, we hit bridal shops across Cairo in the evenings.

It was a strange time. Our shopping excursions sometimes accidentally crossed paths with large demonstrations. The entire city was trembling and stood on a knife's edge as varying fractions struggled to gain power in the aftermath of the revolution. The Muslim Brotherhood and the Salafists had won the first free elections. However, the numerous revolutionaries who had no ties to religion were reluctant to accept the outcome. This was why either one or the other side was always protesting. The turmoil persisted even into June 2012, when the Muslim Brotherhood's Mohammed Mursi was elected President. The old clique around former President Mubarak and the secular forces in the country were reluctant to accept the victory of the Muslim Brotherhood. I was only aware of this through a veil, through my wedding veil. It was much more important for me to reach the registry office with Mahmud.

We finally arrived at that point. Our appointment was scheduled, and a lovely white wedding gown with a train and veil was hanging in my closet. Of course, I didn't show these to Mahmud. He arrived that day in a black suit cut to the waist, looking very elegant. As I climbed out of the taxi, his eyes grew huge. "Do you like it?" I asked.

"What did I ever do to deserve this? I've won the jackpot with you," he replied.

Mahmud held out his arm to me. I almost regretted our decision not to invite any guests as we solemnly stepped into the registry office. We soon found ourselves standing before the registry officer, and both felt embarrassed. "Do you take this man to be your husband?" the man asked me.

"Yes," I breathed.

Mahmud confirmed his will as well. The official declared us man and wife, and then Mahmud lifted my veil and kissed me. Everything was so perfect that it almost felt real. The registry employees who signed our documents as witnesses congratulated us and brought us sweets. I was happy as I left the office at Mahmud's side–and it was somehow hard to distinguish between appearance and reality at that moment.

Later on, Mahmud admitted that as we stepped outside, he had secretly prayed, "Allah, please let her become my actual wife." Similar ideas flashed through my mind, but since we were both rather shy, Mahmud drove me home, and neither of us said anything.

Nonetheless, something changed between us. It was as if the wedding flipped a switch, especially for Mahmud. Of course, he had always been very accommodating and attentive in his interactions with me, but now he was carrying me. Since I was now–at least on paper–his wife, he felt obligated to look after me and ensure I was safe.

For example, whenever he heard that the ruling Muslim Brotherhood's desire to Islamize the laws was stirring up unrest in the neighborhood close to my university, he would call me immediately and ask where I was located. He wanted to prevent me from stumbling into a crowd because something like that could end badly for a woman. Foreign women, in particular, were often harassed or touched inappropriately in such situations. So he would pick me up in his car and take me home if he could somehow arrange it. If he couldn't, he asked me to take a taxi, adding that he would later reimburse me for the expense. It was as if he were my husband. And at some point, I started to wish that he were.

I eagerly waited for him to do something; I didn't dare to attempt anything myself. Whenever he drove me home, I hugged him, and the gleam in his eyes told me he liked this. However, I didn't kiss him. I was worried that he would think I was immodest if I did so. He came from a very religious family, which was probably why he held back so much. It was his way of showing respect to me.

"Mahmud," I said one day when we were sitting together in his car once more, and I was slowly but surely growing desperate because I yearned so much to be close to him. To be physically close to him. "Do you ever wish that we'd had a proper wedding?" Fortunately, it was dark, so he couldn't see how pink I blushed as I asked this.

"Oh, Mihrigul. You're my dream woman," he said. "There's nothing in the world I want more than to truly be married to you." He picked up my hand and kissed it, then suddenly pressed a kiss to my lips. And with that, the spell was broken.

From that moment on, we were a couple. A real couple, I mean: lovers. As the bloody aftermath of the revolution raged outside, we floated along on pink clouds. We spent every free minute with each other, cooing like love birds. We either strolled through the city hand in hand or met up at my apartment, where my friends already knew about us. In a certain sense, I think they realized the potential between Mahmud and myself earlier than we did. At least Aja had the inventor of our marriage. And Tanja also had a serious boyfriend: Erfan, who was also an Uyghur. They had nothing against another man going and coming through our door. And I convinced pious Mahmud that we weren't doing anything wrong because he was my husband. "Yes, indeed I am," he confirmed proudly.

However, we still had one major problem; we hadn't told either set of our parents about our marriage. Thus, for example, Mahmud could never spend the night with me because his mother expected him to return home in the evening. And this also meant that moving in together and trying to start a family was out of the question.

Mahmud insisted that we end our secrecy regarding our families. "I'd like to meet your parents and introduce you to mine," he declared. "I want us all to have a huge wedding celebration."

"That would be lovely," I replied.

I also wanted to have my father's blessing. However, whenever I imagined his reaction to learning that I had secretly married an Arab man, I felt my stomach drop. "Let's not tell my parents everything's a done deal," I suggested to Mahmud.

"What do you propose?"

"I'd like for you to meet my father and for him to give us his blessing to get married freely."

He nodded. "Then this what we should do."

I could hear something in his voice that sounded almost like regret that we had gone about things so unilaterally. In Egypt, it was also customary for a man to ask for consent from his sweetheart's father and for both families to agree. And then the dowry was worked out. Weddings were typically expensive for the groom's family because they had to give gifts of gold jewelry to the bride. The husband also had to prepare the home they would subsequently share. Perhaps Mahmud felt like he was a kind of wedding sneak. However, we couldn't turn back time. We could only try to make good on our hurried, secret marriage and start the whole thing over again.

The next time I called my parents, I invited them to come to Egypt. "I've been living here for almost two years," I said. "Please come and visit me finally!"

"How do you think we could do that?" my father chuckled. He worked as a bus driver. "Do you think I've won the lottery?"

"I can take out a loan from my school for the airline tickets," I lied.

"Ah. And how are you planning on paying it back?"

"That won't be a problem for me! I now have a well-paid job as a translator." In reality, Mahmud would pay for the tickets. "Pleeease!" I added pleadingly. "I miss both of you so much."

My father promised to consider my request. I bombarded him with invitations–and even claimed that the government was promoting tourism to lure back travelers who had been staying away because of the volatile situation. "What difference does it make whether I come to you or you come to me?"

He eventually gave in, but our agreed date was still so far away. Until then, Mahmud and I would have to keep our plans on the back burner. We waited impatiently for their arrival.

My parents came to Cairo in mid-2013. Mahmud drove to the airport with me; I needed him at my side because I was insanely excited about this important meeting. We had planned to introduce our two sets of parents a few days later. Mahmud's father and mother already knew they would be meeting his bride's parents, and they had been preparing carefully for this.

But my father didn't know this when he entered the arrival hall with Menzire. He was a slim, not particularly tall, man. I recognized him instantly due to the traditional fabric hat he always wore to conceal his hair's thinning. In the hustle and bustle of passengers, he looked rather lost. I waved at him. "Mihrigul!" he called happily.

"Baba!"

He hurried toward me, spread his arms, and held me tightly against his chest. "My daughter," he said, "I'm so glad to see you again!"

When he finally let me go, I pointed at Mahmud. "And this is my friend, Mahmud," I declared in introduction.

This was the first moment my father realized that the strange man at my side belonged to me. His expression darkened.

"Hello, Mr. Mahmud," he said with a formal handshake. "It is very nice to meet you."

"My pleasure," Mahmud replied.

"Are you taking classes together?" my father asked in Uyghur.

"Mahmud is my friend."

"Ah."

Mahmud picked up my parents' suitcases and drove into the city. Before taking them to the inn where they would be staying, we ate shish kebabs together. In the restaurant, I watched my father eye Mahmud. "He is a decent boy," he suddenly remarked in Uyghur before asking if he was married.

"No," I replied, "of course not."

"But isn't he Egyptian?"

I nodded, wondering a little about these questions. Besides, I thought talking about Mahmud in front of him was rude, even more so considering that he couldn't understand anything. This was why I asked my father if we could continue this conversation later on in private.

"Well, out with it!" he demanded once we were alone at their inn.

After their long flight, my parents were both exhausted and should have been headed for bed. Instead, my aunt started to get undressed, but my father wanted to discuss this matter first. "What all is going on with this Mahmud? Why did I have to meet him?"

"We want to get married," I declared, letting the facade drop.

"Hmm, I was afraid of that," he said, frowning. My father seemed to be thinking, searching for the right words.

"You said you think he's nice," I reminded him.

"Yes, he's nice, but he's an Arab. And the Arabs and we don't get along well together. We're too different for a marriage to work out. He needs an Arab woman, and you need an Uyghur man who shares your culture and can understand you."

My father didn't say this maliciously, simply calmly and deliberately. I felt like he wanted the best for me. Nonetheless, his words presented an insurmountable hurdle for our relationship—I couldn't accept that.

"Please don't be so hasty, Baba," I pleaded. "We love each other. In three days, you will meet Mahmud's parents, and then you can see if you like his family."

"No, this meeting cannot take place," he declined. "My mind is already made up."

With his firm position, my father put me in a difficult situation. I had expected that it would be difficult for him to accept my choice since we Uyghurs carry a lot of prejudices against the Arabs, mainly in matters that pertain to religion. For example, we accuse them of interpreting Islam too narrowly. In addition, many Uyghurs are offended that Arabs like to act as if they know how to live our religion correctly. This was also true of my father. In his opinion, Arabs were too strict and backward-looking. However, this wasn't fair where Mahmud was concerned. Of course, he came from a devout family, but he was no extremist. Besides, he was my husband. But I couldn't exactly present this as an argument against my father.

I leveraged every bit of eloquence at my disposal until I eventually convinced him to come to the meeting. We had booked a table at an elegant restaurant on the banks of the Nile. Because I knew that Mahmud's family was more conservative, I wrapped a light scarf over my head. "Now you're wearing a turban!" my father commented on my appearance.

"It's perfectly normal in Egypt," I argued as I asked Menzire to follow my example so that we'd make a good impression on my in-laws. "It would be a sign of respect to them." Grumbling, she agreed.

My parents' mood had hit rock bottom when we entered the restaurant, where Mahmud's family was already waiting on us. However, they had dressed up nicely in their own way. Mahmud's father was wearing a beige caftan with gold trim, while his mother was all in black, having donned a beaded abaya and matching hijab. Their appearance contrasted markedly with my parents' clothing, which was more western and modern. My father, who was in slacks and a jacket, raised his eyebrows. "They look so old-fashioned compared to us," he remarked to my aunt in Uyghur.

"Indeed!" she agreed as she snatched the scarf off her head.

Mahmud's family had brought gifts for us. Menzire received an elegant white shawl, and my father was given a caftan in the same shade of beige as the one Mahmud's father was wearing. He rolled his eyes imperceptibly as he accepted the present. Then Mahmud's mother pulled out a small casket in which was nestled a golden ring which she placed solemnly on my finger. Of course, she had been informed that this meeting was an engagement celebration, but this gesture made my father furious. I feared he would storm out of the restaurant in outrage, but he got himself back under control and sat in his seat as if set in concrete.

Our hosts had already ordered. After the gifts had been given, the waiters immediately materialized, carrying out everything the kitchen had to offer: various kinds of meat, hummus, pickled peppers, stuffed grape leaves, baked eggplant, tabouleh, lentil salad, olives, a spicy garlic sauce, and fish from the Nile. They served the dishes on numerous small plates placed in the center of the table so that everyone could serve themselves. My mother-in-law constantly offered us something to eat, but I was so tense that I could hardly choke down a bite. And my parents declared that they weren't all that hungry. They just sat there with stony expressions. "What is wrong with them? Are they feeling poorly?" my mother-in-law eventually asked in desperation. Unfortunately, she could not speak with them because of the language barrier.

"They're just tired," I offered as an excuse.

"From their trip?"

"Yes, they're still struggling with the time difference."

"That's understandable." She gazed at me sadly, and I wished that the ground would swallow me up, so ashamed was I of my parents and their impossible behavior.

After the horrible meeting, it was clear that Mahmud's and my plans wouldn't have a happy ending. My father was irate, and he forbade me to have any further contact with Mahmud. "That's enough, Mihrigul," he declared bluntly. "You will not be marrying that man. You won't marry any Arab, do you understand?"

"You're being terribly unfair!"

"I'm not being unfair at all. I only want what's best for you. And then there's the fact that these people are strangers to us; their culture is completely different from our own. That could *never* end well."

"But Mahmud is the only man I'd ever want!"

"Hogwash!" he cut me off. "You will marry an Uyghur man." My father continued declaring that he intended to take me home with them when they left. "It's obvious that the only thing you're getting here is dumb ideas."

I thought I had to be mishearing things. "You want me to break off my studies?"

"No," my father asserted. "I'm simply a realist. The next Mahmud is probably waiting around the corner. I'm not crazy enough to leave you here on your own!"

I began to cry. First, he forbade me from seeing Mahmud, and now he wanted to take me away from my studies. I begged him to reconsider his decision. "You'll destroy my career!"

"No, you're the one destroying your career," he countered. "You're to blame for all of this."

He remained adamant. After dropping my parents off back at their inn, I went home and wept the whole evening and night. I wasn't in any state to even respond to Mahmud's texts. After all, what could I possibly say to him? That I had to break off everything with him because my father refused to accept him as a son-in-law? That I had to return to Xinjiang?

At some point, there was a knock at my door. "What happened?" my Spanish friend Tanja asked as she walked over to my bed in her nightgown.

I told her about the disaster that had arisen when we tried to introduce our families to each other. "My father is dead set against our relationship. He has even forbidden me to stay in Egypt!"

Tanja was shocked. "You can't let him do that, Mihrigul!" she said. "You aren't fifteen anymore, and he can't just force you to go back home with him."

"But I can't go against my father's wishes. I just can't!" I tried to explain to her how important parental consent and authority were in my culture.

"Then give him what he wants: marry an Uyghur man who lives in Egypt." She grinned mischievously. I had no clue what she found so funny in all of this.

"I'm already married to Mahmud," I reminded her.

"Yes, you married him in the eyes of the state, but you could at least stage an Islamic ceremony for your father's sake."

I gazed at her uncomprehendingly. If I had an Uyghur husband in Cairo, my father would surely let me remain here.

"I know a candidate who doesn't have any high expectations when it comes to marriage," Tanja continued as her grin grew a little wider than before. I was still tottering on the line. "Erfan, of course!" she resolved the riddle. My friend was speaking of her Uyghur boyfriend. I was speechless.

"Tanja…!" Could she be serious?

"Well, it makes all the sense in the world. The two of you agree to a sham marriage, and all of your problems will be solved." It sounded too good to be true. "It'll all be fine. I'll speak to Erfan first thing in the morning," she promised.

The following morning, Tanja asked Erfan to come over. My fellow student sat with us at our kitchen table for half an hour as we explained my dire situation to him. "These damned stubborn Uyghurs!" he exclaimed. Erfan was a classmate of mine, and he thought my father's desire to take me away from the university was unfair. "Should I talk to him?"

"We had something else in mind," Tanja replied.

She filled him in on our plans. I blushed crimson as I listened to her, and even Erfan's chin dropped. He was a fairly self-assured and confident fellow, but he had never thought his girlfriend or I capable of cooking up a plan as audacious as this.

Tanja saw him wavering, which was why she pressed harder. "I think Mihrigul's father deserves nothing less than this deception," she said, reaffirming her position.

"Yes, that's true," Erfan said doubtfully.

"Pleeease, Erfan! We can't let him pack her into a suitcase and drag her back to Xinjiang. We don't live in the Middle Ages, after all!"

He nodded thoughtfully.

"I knew it. You're a sweetheart!" she crowed, pressing a kiss to his lips. And just like that, the matter was settled. Erfan had hooked himself on the job, although he didn't look delighted at the outcome. However, he was now involved, for better or for worse. I was sure he wasn't doing this for my sake, but he wished to please his girlfriend.

A few days later, he went to see my father, who was more than a little astonished that I had landed a replacement candidate for Mahmud so quickly. My father was over the moon! He would finally get the Uyghur son-in-law he had been dreaming of. He even happened to know Erfan's father and was friends with him. So he had no reservations whatsoever about agreeing to this arrangement, especially since the family had a good reputation.

"Erfan is a marvelous choice!" he congratulated me as we entered the mosque where we would marry. Once again, the wedding was to occur within a very small group, without a wedding party. And this caused a strange sense of deja-vu within me; I was painfully reminded of my first marriage and could hardly believe it. This was my second time going through a marriage of convenience in my short life. And all because I wanted to stay in Cairo and finish my studies. I wondered if what I was doing was selfish. Could there have been some other preferable solution?

More than anything else, I was in anguish at the thought of Mahmud, who naturally wouldn't be at the ceremony. I felt dreadful for him since, due to my profound disappointment, I hadn't been in a condition to talk to him since our disastrous meeting at the restaurant. It took almost a week for me to find the strength to call and inform him that my parents refused to approve of our relationship. "I'm so sorry, but they won't accept you as my husband. I can't see you anymore because of that," I had declared.

After all the effort that he had invested in me, he was understandably very disappointed. And it also broke my heart to be the cause of such terrible despair.

"I'm going to marry Erfan," I added, "of course, just for appearance's sake. There's going to be a ceremony at the mosque…." I was about to explain to him that I was only doing this because otherwise, my father was going to force me to travel home with him, but I never got that far. My words so injured Mahmud that he hung up.

That evening, I received a text from him. "As of today, you are dead to me," it said. This was the last thing I heard from him. He changed his number soon after that.

I was extremely sad, but I understood his bitterness and told myself I had to accept his decision. He had the right to end this chapter of his life and forget about me. However, only a short time later, I discovered I was pregnant.

CHAPTER 3

Three Times a Mother

As soon as I woke up in the mornings, I felt sick, so sick that I had to immediately jump out of bed and dash to the bathroom to throw up.

Hey, Mihrigul, are you already back in there?" Tanja asked me in surprise one day when I once again occupied the bathroom for hours, afraid to get too far from the toilet. I eventually emerged from the room, chalky white, and staggered back to my room. "Are you sick or something?" she called after me.

Later, when we were sitting at the breakfast table with Erfan, she studied me as I picked at the omelet she had fixed. I felt hungry, of course, but could eat next to nothing because the smell turned my stomach.

"Say, there's something wrong, isn't it?" Tanja said. "Don't you just want to go get checked out by a doctor?"

She asked my "husband," Erfan, to take me to the Behman Hospital. When I described my symptoms to a doctor here, she immediately had a suspicion. "Have you had sexual intercourse in the past few months?"

I blushed in the face of such a direct question. My gut reaction was to shake my head, but then I thought about Mahmud, calculated back to the last time I had seen him and nodded sheepishly.

"And when was your last period?"

I thought about this. "About three months ago."

She smiled. "Then we need to do a pregnancy test urgently."

Although the chance of being pregnant was an obvious conclusion, I had never even considered this possibility. Yes, I was literally shocked when the doctor recommended the test. Pregnant! Good heavens, no! I was living by myself in a foreign country. There was no way I could have a child at this point.

"Just relax," the doctor said after watching me for a moment. "A pregnancy is good news. Of course, it is a big change for any woman. But this might not be what's going on. We'll know in a little while."

She asked me for a urine sample. Then I was supposed to go into the hallway and sit on a bench. I broke out in a cold sweat as I waited along with Erfan on the test results. "No, dear God, please don't send me a child," I prayed.

After a while, the doctor called me back into her room. With a grin, she held out her hand to me. "Congratulations, Mrs. Tursun," she said. "You're pregnant."

I gazed at her, completely bewildered and had no idea how to react. "This can't be true," was the only thing I could think. This was a wicked, wicked trick of fate.

The doctor led me to another room for an ultrasound. I took my place, trembling. "If we're lucky, we'll be able to see the baby." she declared as she inserted the transducer into my vagina. I secretly hoped that wouldn't happen. Perhaps the woman had made a mistake, and everything would prove to be a misunderstanding.

"Oh, this is exciting!" she suddenly cried out, pointing at the screen where a pair of circular, gray shapes appeared. They were so blurry that I could hardly make out anything.

"Do you see a baby?" I asked fearfully.

"Yes, Mrs. Tursun. Two of them."

I was distraught by the time I left the hospital. Erfan drove me home to Tanja, and I told her about the catastrophic diagnosis. Aja was also there for the conversation. "If Mahmud and I hadn't split up, this would be the most wonderful thing I could imagine for myself," I admitted. "But not now!"

"Now things are more complicated," Tanja declared.

"But they're not hopeless," Aja claimed, lapsing into thought for a moment. "We could hunt up Mahmud and explain the situation to him.

"I could speak with him," Erfan offered.

But I didn't think this was a good idea; Mahmud had cut me out of his life, and I could understand why. In the end, I broke his heart. Now that I found myself in dire straits, it was impossible for me to crawl back to him. I had no idea how to do that, even if I wanted to. I didn't even have his phone number anymore. And when I had recently driven past his shop on the bus, I noticed a new sign hanging there. His regret had driven him to fold his tents in Cairo.

"I can't have these children," I declared firmly. There was no point in wasting more anguish over this; it was simply too much for me to cope with in my current situation. "I'll have an abortion."

Aja looked skeptical, but Tanja understood my decision immediately. "It would probably be for the best," she remarked.

"What is the legal situation in Egypt anyway?" I asked Aja. "Are abortions permitted here?"

"No, only for health reasons."

"Hmm…" Tanja wrinkled her brow as she thought. "But Mihrigul is having twins… Couldn't that be considered problematic?"

"Definitely for such a small, delicate woman as Mihrigul," Aja agreed. "In any case, if they wished to, the doctors could maybe establish a legitimate justification for an abortion."

Thank God, I thought. There seemed to be a potential way out for me. "Then all we have to do is find a willing doctor."

I suggested inquiring at the hospital. Since abortion was a fairly common practice in China, I didn't think anything about this. However, Aja shook her head doubtfully. "You shouldn't go back there," she warned. "It would be smarter for us to find out the name of someone who might be open to this course of action ahead of time." She promised to ask around.

Although she tried for several days, she came to no satisfactory conclusions—all the tips she received related to quacks plying their trade in dubious back alley clinics. I wasn't ready to run that risk.

Therefore, after a week, I made another appointment at the hospital. The obstetrician who examined me confirmed his colleague's finding that I was carrying twins. The man squinted before declaring, "It might even be triplets."

"What?!!" With that, my courage evaporated.

"At this stage, it's hard to tell for certain. In any case, this pregnancy won't be easy for you."

I felt that my diagnosis was worsening with each doctor's visit. It's now, or never, I thought. I had to ask him to end my nightmare. "Doctor," I began, noticing my high and squeaky voice. "Is there perhaps another possibility?"

He looked at me, puzzled over what I was getting at. "Of course, we'll assist you with anesthesia."

"I don't want to have these children."

He smiled indulgently. "It is completely normal that you're nervous. Don't worry too much. Other women have brought multiples into the world."

"I would like to end this pregnancy," I declared bluntly.

"Ah, really?" He frowned. "What does your husband say about this?"

45

"He, uh…"

"You're married, aren't you?"

"Yes." I nodded uncertainly. Technically speaking, I had two husbands, but according to the authorities and my ID card, Mahmud was my husband. My religious marriage to Erfan hadn't changed that bit of information.

"If you wish to terminate your pregnancy, then your spouse must give his consent."

"Really?" I gazed at him in astonishment.

"Yes. You must both come here and bring your personal ID and a copy of your marriage license."

"But that can't be," I stammered. He shot me a questioning look. "My husband lives abroad."

"That doesn't change anything. If you wish to have an abortion, you must ask him to return to provide his consent. Otherwise, there's nothing I can do for you." The doctor shrugged. "That's the law here in Egypt."

When I left the office, I understood that my status as Mahmud's wife presented a veritable problem for me; I could no longer make decisions about my body on my own. I found this quite shocking, perhaps because I came from a country where abortions were viewed as little more than a routine procedure. A Chinese woman who accidentally became pregnant and wished to end the situation booked an appointment with a doctor, paid the operation fees, and had the fetus removed. This was no major act, and a woman could make this decision alone; she didn't need anyone's consent. On the other hand, Egyptian law compelled me to bear the children growing inside me until Mahmud released me from this obligation.

There was only one thing to do: I had to go back home to my parents and have the procedure done there. Later on, once I had taken care of everything, I could still try to return to Egypt to complete my studies. If I didn't do something, I wouldn't be able to do this anyway. It would be impossible to keep up with my studies and care for three infants as a single mother.

I called my father. After the whole charade with which I had deceived him, this was anything but easy for me. However, I knew there was no way out; he had to help me escape my predicament. "Papa!"

"Mihrigul, my child!" he exclaimed delightedly as he caught sight of my face on his phone screen. "How are both of you doing?"

"Both? Oh, fine, I mean." I didn't have enough strength to pretend. "Actually, not good at all," I managed.

"Why? What's wrong?"

"I'm pregnant."

"But that's wonderful! Congratulations to both of you!"

"Papa, it's not how you think…." How could I explain this to him? "Erfan's not the father."

"Ah." His face darkened. "Who is?" He probably already suspected what was coming next."

"Mahmud is," I admitted to him—and waited for the angry outburst. I was prepared to face his fury, but my father was silent. This was almost worse.

"Papa, I'm so terribly sorry…." I started to weep. "But you shouldn't think that I'm an adulteress. It happened before my betrothal to Erfan. I was no longer a virgin, so I shouldn't have married him. That was to appease you…."

The more I said, the more speechless my father became on the other end.

"I'm having triplets—and I need to have an abortion…."

He shook his head in disbelief. "What have you done, Mihrigul?" he sighed.

My father was so shocked by my confession that he asked for time to think. I could understand this and felt incredibly ashamed of my behavior toward him. What had gotten me into all this? Why had I made so many bad decisions? I never should have gone behind his back and married Mahmud without his consent. But now it was too late for regret; I had to live with the consequences of my actions.

I impatiently waited for him to call me back, but my father needed to move at his own pace. After all that I had done, would he be prepared to help me? Or would he tell me that I had to muddle through my future alone? I could hardly bear the time I had to wait for this news.

Finally, after three long days, my phone buzzed. "Listen, Mihrigul," he said. "Menzire and I have been talking...." I saw my aunt appear in the background of my screen. "Here are our thoughts on the matter: We're a family and help each other out." I felt a warmth start to pulse through me.

"And so, get on a plane and come back to us. But don't come to abort the babies. I want you to keep them and let us raise them."

"Papa!" I said, touched.

"Your brother and his wife still have no children. They could take one of the little ones," Menzire suggested.

I was completely overwhelmed and had no idea what I should say.

"And don't tell that Arab anything about them, alright?" my father demanded. "We want to raise them our way."

I smiled at this condition. However, I was infinitely grateful that he could show me such kindness after our conflict and my numerous lies and even offered to take care of my children. I couldn't refuse. "Thank you, Papa," I murmured. "I'll bring them to Qarqan so that they can become Uyghur children."

After deciding to keep my children, I looked at the world with different eyes. Suddenly I no longer felt all alone. I was no longer responsible for myself but for three other human beings who completely depended on my protection and decisions.

This insight lent new weight to all of my actions, and my priorities shifted radically. Before this point, I had subordinated everything to my goal of continuing my studies and graduating with distinction, but now my health moved to the forefront. My most important task was to bring these three children into the world, hale and healthy. And to do that, I had to be prepared to make compromises regarding other matters.

This became clear to me when I wanted to finalize my travel plans. My original plan had been to return home to my parents as quickly as possible to have my children there. However, this didn't turn out to be so simple, with triplets growing inside of me.

"I must strenuously urge you not to travel," my obstetrician urged me when I inquired about the risks posed to me by such a long flight home in my condition. Air China had already flatly refused to transport me, and Egypt Air was only willing to do so if I accepted all liability for this decision.

I felt torn. Should I get on board an airplane? I had reached my fifth month by this time, and my girth had grown considerably because of the triplets. I could also feel the strain in my day-to-day life: I could no longer move as easily, was constantly tired, and wished for nothing more than to be close to my family. In Egypt, I suddenly felt out of place and vulnerable. I didn't know how I was supposed to get through what I was facing all by myself.

"Mihrigul, I know that you no longer feel at home in Cairo, but you shouldn't take any risks," my father urged during one of our next phone calls. "It would be better for you to be patient and to have the children there."

"All by myself?" I protested self-pityingly.

"I'll ask Menzire if she can be with you for this."

And that was how it came about: a short time later, my aunt landed again in Cairo, this time without my father. She was going to help take care of me during the final stage of my pregnancy and be by my side for the birth, which the doctors had told me wouldn't be easy.

I was very grateful when Menzire moved into our apartment. We stayed in the same room, and she slept on a narrow mattress next to my bed. She promised to also cook for me. "It is very important that you eat well during your pregnancy, so the children receive the nutrients they need," she explained. And I believed her since she had brought two children into the world herself. Besides, I was seriously craving traditional Uyghur cuisine.

The following day, we went together to the market to pick up lamb meat, chilis, parsley, cumin, and yogurt. We seared the meat in a pan, seasoned it heartily, and mixed the yogurt with the herbs. I also baked naan bread according to the recipe I had learned from my grandmother. My aunt praised me. "You cook wonderfully!"

I modestly nodded because it was true. I learned how to cook early on from my grandmother, who had also been Menzire's mother. I wished I could return the compliment, but that would have been a lie. Menzire had no clue when it came to cooking because that task had fallen to her sisters at home. As a result, she couldn't prepare chicken or fish properly and didn't even like our traditional lamb and rice dishes. If my aunt had gotten things her way, we would probably have eaten noodles daily.

And so I took over cooking for us. I jotted down the ingredients my aunt should purchase and fixed our meals. I soon realized that I also had to take care of most of the housework. This proved exhausting because my body was so out of shape by this point. After eating, I usually needed to lie down. I soon lost all desire to go out because everything was so stressful. My aunt had little sympathy for this; she wished to experience Cairo. She was undeterred by the politically tense situation and the precarious safety environment on the streets. "Nothing will happen to us. Come on, let's go on a little shopping trip," she often suggested. However, I always said no.

Of course, this resulted in some tension. My aunt was bored, and I felt obligated to keep my "guest" entertained. Her presence didn't result in the intended relief but, on the contrary, in an additional burden for me. After we had spent a few weeks together, I could no longer take it. "Listen, Menzire," I said to her. "I think I'll be fine here on my own." However, I knew that there was nothing she desired more either than to be done with our experiment. "What would you think about returning home to prepare everything for the children and me?" I suggested.

It didn't take me long to convince her. "Are you sure you can handle all this alone?" she asked hopefully.

"Sure, no problem," I lied.

"And if you need anything else, you'll let me know, okay?"

A deep sigh escaped me as Menzire departed. Relieved, I watched the airport bus drive away until I could no longer see it. I finally no longer had to worry about her. Now there was just me and my own needs. On my way home, I purchased half a chicken and cooked it into a soup back at the apartment. I slowly and thoughtfully consumed it and then stretched out to sleep. Glorious, I thought.

For a while, I did alright on my own. I ate well, slept a lot, and even slowly began to get excited about the babies. What would it feel like to hold three babies in my arms at one time? What would they look like? Would they resemble Mahmud more or me?

I went to the hospital every week for a checkup, where the doctors observed my pregnancy very closely. The more my stomach swelled up, the more concerned they grew that all four of us could safely make it through my pregnancy. My delicate frame wasn't built for such a burden, and even walking became increasingly difficult. I immediately broke out in a sweat whenever I climbed the steps to my apartment. I could hardly drag myself to the hospital and back for my checkups.

The doctors eventually put me on full bed rest. They feared that I would risk premature labor if I didn't stay off my feet for the last few weeks of my pregnancy. I didn't know how in the world I could make this work. "How are you imagining this will function?" I asked my obstetrician, Doctor Nur.

"If you don't have anyone at home who can care for you, I'll need to admit you to the hospital," he replied. I considered this for a moment, then nodded. This option struck me as preferable to entrusting my care to my flatmates.

Starting early in my eighth month, I was a resident of the Behman Hospital. My stomach continued to grow. At some point, I consisted only of my stomach, and I thought I would explode if I grew even one more centimeter. Dr. Nur watched my development with concern. At the end of my first week in the hospital, he sat beside my bed to discuss an important matter.

"Mrs. Tursun, we will do everything in our power to support you during delivery. But it definitely won't be easy...."

I was already aware of this, so I wondered what Dr. Nur was trying to tell me with this line of commentary.

"... you need to be prepared for everything...."

I nodded.

"Do you have any relatives in Egypt whom we could notify in an emergency?"

I shook my head.

"But that is extremely important, Mrs. Tursun," he declared with a serious look on his face. "I don't wish to frighten you, and I'm so sorry to need to speak with you so directly about this, but there is a chance that you won't survive the delivery."

I gazed at him in astonishment. So this was what the doctor had wanted to get out in the open.

"Are you still in contact with the father of your children?"

"No..." I stammered.

"Please listen to me. It is very important that you reach out to him again so that if the unthinkable happens, your children aren't left without any family. You know what that would mean...."

I lowered my eyes. Yes, damn it, I knew. Suddenly everything was crystal clear. If I didn't inform Mahmud of my situation and convince him to acknowledge these children as his, they would land in an orphanage if anything happened to me. Since my own family lived in another country, they would have no way of taking the babies to live with them.

The thought of this horrified me; I couldn't close my eyes for even a moment that night. However, there was no way to explain away the danger. It was a real possibility that I wouldn't survive the delivery. That fact didn't bother me, but the thought that my babies would be left completely unprotected without either father or mother was unbearable. There was no way I could do that to them. But should I attempt to contact Mahmud? "As of today, you are dead to me." I could still envision his last text to me.

When Tanja and Erfan visited me in the hospital the following day, she immediately noticed that I had dark rings underneath my eyes. "You poor dear, you probably can't sleep anymore," Tanja exclaimed with a glance at my stomach. "No wonder. You're hauling around that ball."

A deep sigh escaped me. "I wish that was the reason."

"What's going on?"

I told Tanja about the conversation with the doctor. Her eyes grew huge when I got to the part about the possibility I might not survive the delivery. "The doctor even wants me to sign a proviso that if in doubt, the children's lives should be saved before mine."

"Good grief!" she exclaimed.

"That's not a problem," I assured her. "I will sign that for my children. My only concern is what will happen to them if I'm no longer there. I don't have any family here."

"But you have Aja and me." She glanced at Erfan. "And..."

"No," he interrupted her. "Mihrigul's right! The children have to grow up with their families. And they have a family here in Egypt. We need to speak with Mahmud."

I gazed at him uncertainly. I was thinking about my parents, who had made me promise to leave Mahmud out of this. And then I thought about the text message again.

"But, Mihrigul!" Erfan persisted in dead earnestness. "You have a responsibility to your children. If you do happen to die, you can't leave them to their fate."

Tears welled in my eyes. "You don't think I know that?" I snapped at him.

"But of course, and that is why we must notify Mahmud–so he can assume the responsibility in a worst-case scenario. For the well-being of your children."

It wasn't as if this thought had never entered my mind during the months of my pregnancy. "But I have no idea how to contact him!" I bemoaned. "He changed his number."

"Will you let me search for him?"

I nodded weakly. "All right," I said.

I first sent Erfan to Mahmud's clothing shop, which no longer belonged to him, as I had suspected. Erfan learned from the new owner that Mahmud had moved abroad. The owner didn't have his new address, and Mahmud had also changed his email address. My hope of finding him sank. However, there was one last possibility; my ID still bore his parents' address.

Erfan went by there, introducing himself as an old friend of Mahmud's and asking his father for Mahmud's new contract information. "Mahmud recently started a new job in Dubai. He was hired on by a trading company there," Erfan explained upon his return to the hospital. My heart started to pound.

"Were you able to speak to him?"

"Yes. I had to try a couple of times, though, because he didn't recognize my number. He eventually picked up, though."

"And?"

"I told him everything." Erfan sounded cautious. "He said that he needs time to think things through."

"I understand." This didn't sound promising.

"Don't give up yet. Be patient, Mihrigul."

After Erfan's report, I felt rather somber. Mahmud was still quite hurt by my actions and reluctant to shift his perspective. However, his reasoning made complete sense to me. How could it be any different? What could I have hoped for by letting the man whom Mahmud probably viewed as a rival call and inform him that I was expecting triplets? How would I have responded in his place?

My health went into a steady decline. There were two reasons for this. First of all, my body was producing an inadequate quantity of blood, which required me to have multiple transfusions. Secondly, the three babies had grown too large for my body. The doctors decided they would need to induce labor during my 31st week and take the babies by C-section. Things weren't looking all that great for me.

"We will do everything within our power for you," Dr. Nur promised me, "However, I cannot guarantee anything. Life-and-death decisions are made by Allah, not by me."

A few minutes after the doctor departed, I saw a magnificent, colorful bouquet appeared in my doorway. Behind it was hidden a man, who stopped at my threshold. "May I come in?" I heard Mahmud's voice come from behind the flowers.

I was unable to speak as tears trickled down my cheeks. "Mahmud!" I whispered as he stepped closer. "I'm so glad that you're here!"

"As am I!" He hugged me shyly, smelling as good as always, like aftershave. Mahmud also had tears in his eyes. "Why didn't you tell me?"

"I didn't know how you would react."

"I'm so sorry you've had to go through all this alone!"

We lay in each other's arms and wept. Mahmud assured me that he was overjoyed that I was pregnant and wanted nothing in the world more than to be a father. However, one question was still burning in his soul.

"Are you quite sure that… ?" he began, turning red.

I immediately knew what he was getting at. "A thousand percent," I declared firmly. "I have never slept with any man but you,

Mahmud. The ceremony with Erfan was only arranged for my father's benefit. We were never a real couple."

Mahmud lowered his eyes and said nothing. I sensed he wanted to believe me, but he wasn't convinced.

"If you like, we can arrange for a DNA test right after the delivery. Then you can be sure the children are yours," I suggested. He beamed.

"Good," he said.

"But until then, you'll have to trust me."

"I do," he agreed.

With Mahmud at my side, I suddenly felt strong. I was ready to get on with the delivery; Mahmud promised to stay with me the whole time. This gave me new strength, but above all, I was reassured by the thought that he would be there for our children if I didn't survive the operation. For this, I was boundlessly grateful to him.

Before the doctors administered the anesthesia for the C-section, we made several videos. In one of them, I repeated my agreement that, in case of doubt, my children's lives should be saved before my own. In a different one, I recorded a message to my parents, informing them of my decision and asking them not to undertake any legal proceedings against the doctors if things went badly.

After that, I felt calm. When the anesthesiologist arrived to give me the injection, Mahmud sat beside me, and I smiled at him. Next, I felt the prick in my arm and watched as the contents of the vial were drained. I then drifted into unconsciousness.

I only know what happened after that from stories and the videos that Mahmud made during the delivery. At first, everything went according to plan. The doctors created an incision in my abdomen, at which I began to bleed profusely, as can be seen in the video. However, they were able to bring all three children safely into the world. First up was Mohammed, the largest and strongest of the three. He was followed by my daughter, Elena. And the caboose was my youngest son Moez, who was much smaller and weaker than his two older siblings.

Once he was born, also safe and sound, Mahmud sighed in relief. In the video, one can see him thank Allah for his healthy children.

However, the doctors in the delivery room seemed to grow increasingly frantic because the triple birth had taken a lot of time, during which I had bled continuously. I had bled too much. Suddenly the monitor flat-lined, and my heart stopped. The video captures my husband's desperate appeal to the doctors to save my life. And with that, the video ends abruptly.

The doctors tried to resuscitate me, but that didn't work. My heartbeat wouldn't start back up again. My body was too weak from the stress it had been through. They thought I was gone and asked Mahmud to shut my eyes. He picked up our oldest son Mohammed, held him up to my face, and said: "Kiss your mother goodbye, little Mohammed, then we'll close her eyes."

The baby touched my cheek–and started to scream. It might sound strange, but somehow I heard his sobs in my mind. The anguished cries of my child were like a wake-up call for me. My body suddenly remembered everything, mainly that my children needed me. I gasped for air, and my heart began to beat once more.

The doctors instantly started resuscitation and administered oxygen to me. I finally woke up under the oxygen mask they strapped over my face.

This was like a miracle for all of us. "I've never seen anything like this in my entire career," the doctor who watched me wake up declared. "You're so small, and you'd lost so much blood. We were starting to think you wouldn't make it, but you're very strong."

"My brave Mihrigul," murmured Mahmud, sitting beside me. He picked up my hand and kissed it.

"How are the babies?" I wanted him to tell me right away. Even as I was waking up, I could still hear my son's sobs, which I had somehow registered in the world between life and death.

"All three of them are healthy."

"And where are they?"

"They're asleep in the neighboring room. Are you ready to meet them?" What kind of question was that?! Mahmud looked at the doctor–and he nodded. He signaled to the nurse, who fetched the triplets.

Shortly after that, the door opened, and two nurses entered carrying the newborns. They laid the oldest, Mohammed, across my chest, and the other two were placed on either side of my head. I thought I was dreaming and could hardly comprehend my happiness.

I cautiously touched the wrinkled faces of my children, who looked astonishingly well-developed despite having been born prematurely. They even had hair on their little heads. Specifically, they had dark, black curls, exactly like their father. And their eyes were also the same dark shade as his. They were the spitting image of him. Mahmud watched me as I saw the babies for the first time and examined them. And the same thoughts were passing through his mind.

"We can save the money on the DNA test," he remarked with a chuckle. "The three of them look like tiny copies of me."

CHAPTER 4

Return to the Unknown

Mahmud was enraptured by his children. During the first few weeks, when I was still recovering from my strenuous delivery, he took care of us around the clock. He turned out to be a loving and responsible father, and everything finally seemed to be going well for us. The possibility of us staying together and raising our children was now completely within the realm of my imagination.

Mahmud's parents were also over the moon when they were told they had grandchildren. To spare their feelings, he had never informed them that my parents had rejected them all those months ago. In their eyes, Mahmud and I had been engaged the entire time–and the only thing he had failed to do was tell them about my pregnancy. However, they now insisted that we celebrate our wedding in some major way. They wanted us to give them a concrete date.

If it had been up to Mahmud, we would have mailed out invitations right away, but I still had something to take care of. "Listen,"

I told him, "you know that I promised my parents I would bring the babies to them. And I need to keep this promise. Then, after that, we can celebrate our wedding."

He nodded in understanding and looked concerned as if he felt uncertain if I would return to him.

"Want to come home with me?" I asked.

He beamed. "Of course, I'll come along with you and the babies!"

In May 2015, six weeks after the triplets were born, we found ourselves sitting together on an airplane to Beijing. I was so happy that Mahmud was accompanying me, especially since I'd had no real idea how to handle the long journey with three infants. This way, we could share the childcare duties. I carried our oldest child when we boarded, while Mahmud carried the two younger ones. And whenever I needed to nurse one or the other of them during the flight, he took care of the other two.

The flight went better than expected; the babies only cried a little at the beginning of our journey. Since they were so small, they slept a lot. Nonetheless, we still felt exhausted when we landed in Beijing after thirteen hours in the air. And this wasn't even our final destination! We would catch a connecting flight to Ürümqi, and from there, we would take a bus through the desert to Qarqan.

As I walked along the concourses of the Beijing airport with Mahmud, my eyes grew huge. After being gone for several years, everything around me felt astonishingly clean and oversized. What a huge building this was! And so modern in comparison to what Egypt had to offer. You could tell at first glance that China was currently in the fast lane. Would my home in Xinjiang also look like this?

I had spent the whole time on the plane wondering what it would be like to face my parents with Mahmud in tow. I hadn't admitted to them that I had contacted him in my moment of need and that we were now a complete family. This wasn't, after all, a topic to discuss on the phone.

I imagined the meeting with them going something like this: I would first enter the house alone with the children to get the lay of the land, so to speak. Then, once I had explained and confessed everything to them, Mahmud would join us. This time, they couldn't simply reject him. After all, he was the babies' father. Even my incorrigible father would have to see that the five of us belonged together. Hopefully, he wouldn't make this too difficult for us.

We finally reached the passport control counter. "May I please see your passports?" the woman at the desk asked, and we presented our documents to her. I had my Chinese passport, Mahmud had his Egyptian passport, and pasted inside was his Chinese visa. The babies also had Egyptian passports. The woman, who was Han Chinese, inspected everything closely and then nodded.

"Will you be staying in Beijing or traveling to another destination?" she asked me. "If so, I need to see your tickets."

I handed over the boarding cards for our connecting flight to Ürümqi.

"Ah, Ürümqi," she said. "And you want to travel there together?"

"Yes, of course," I replied, puzzled by her question. Considering the stroller, it should have been obvious to her that we were traveling together. "We're here to visit my family," I added.

She typed something into her computer, and a shadow flitted over her face. She cleared her throat. "I regret to inform you that this visit will not be possible."

"What do you mean?"

"Only you are allowed to fly out there."

I thought she was joking. "Only me? But why?!"

The woman hemmed and hawed. "Didn't they talk to him at the embassy?"

"No."

"Foreigners aren't allowed to travel to Xinjiang."

I stared at her, open-mouthed. When on earth had these rules gone into effect? "Are you telling me that we bought our tickets for nothing?"

61

"I'm sorry. You should have asked before." The woman lowered her eyes.

"What is going on?" Mahmud asked since we had carried on this conversation in Chinese.

I told him the woman didn't want to allow him and the children to continue our journey. "What?!" he exclaimed angrily. "This can't be happening!"

By this point, we were no longer alone. Two security personnel approached the counter and took Mahmud and me aside so the woman could continue processing the other passengers. "I am sorry that you did not receive this information before now," one of the uniformed men said to Mahmud in English. "But at this time, trips to Xinjiang are only being allowed on special visas."

"But my wife is Chinese. She wants to introduce her parents to our children."

The men conferred with each other. They finally declared that I could continue our trip with the babies.

"But you can see my wife can't travel alone with the children!" Mahmud argued.

"If you like, we can arrange a travel companion to accompany them."

"Really?" he asked in astonishment.

"Yes, we'll take care of it," they promised–and Mahmud capitulated.

"You should travel on your own to see your parents," he told me. "It would be better to choke on just one ticket instead of all five."

"Are you sure?"

"Yes." His eyes glistened, but he didn't want to be the reason why I couldn't see my parents and introduce them to the babies. As the grandparents, he believed they had a right to meet their grandchildren, and he wanted to honor that conviction. He went up in my esteem, especially considering they hadn't treated him well at their first meeting. At that moment, I loved him more than ever. Under the officers' watchful eyes, I pressed a kiss to his lips.

"I will wait for you in Cairo and will think of you every day," Mahmud said in farewell.

"It won't be long. We'll be heading back to you very soon," I promised him. Nonetheless, my heart dropped as I turned around and headed in the other direction with our three children.

Two people were waiting on me at the gate, a Chinese man and a young woman. When they caught sight of me approaching with the children, they hurried toward me and introduced themselves as Mr. Tian and Ms. Cai. "We were told that you need our assistance?" Herr Tian said. He must have received that information from the officers.

The fact that they wanted to be helpful was, at first, a positive thing, in my opinion. Besides, I did need assistance, so I didn't ask any further questions. "This is very nice of you," was all I said.

Mr. Tian and Ms. Cai each picked up one of the children. "Aren't they sweet little mice!" exclaimed Ms. Cai, who was now carrying my daughter Elena. The woman's awkwardness with her revealed that she hadn't carried many infants before now.

We boarded the flight to Ürümqi and took our seats, which had somehow been mysteriously reassigned so that we were all sitting in a single row. I was given the middle seat. It was all a little strange, but I didn't question it. I was much too busy with the babies, whom I needed to nurse one after the other because they had gotten hungry. After that, I dozed off, exhausted, with Mohammed on my lap.

I woke up to the loudspeaker announcement that we had started our descent to Ürümqi. It took me a moment to get my bearings. I wondered who the two people were sitting next to me and why they were holding my children, but then I remembered everything and smiled at Ms. Cai.

However, her expression had changed; Ms. Cai was no longer smiling. Instead, she pulled an identification card from her jacket pocket and held it under my nose. Her name wasn't Cai, but I recognized her photo with the police seal next to it. She was a plainclothes officer. Mr. Tai similarly revealed himself – and from this point on, the two of them dropped all pretense of being friendly towards me. Instead, they spoke dictatorially and gave me orders: "You will get off this plane with us quietly, without saying a word to anyone," they declared.

"But…"

"But nothing!" Mr. Tian interrupted. "You are not allowed to ask any more questions. You will not speak unless you have been spoken to. Understood?"

I nodded, frightened.

Once the plane landed, we got off, and I mutely followed the two officers, who were still carrying my children, Moez and Elena. I had a terrible feeling that I was completely powerless. They led me past the line of passengers waiting at the passport counter to a separate room. Other officers were waiting there; some wore Chinese uniforms, while others were in Uyghur ones.

One of the Uyghur officers gestured for me to sit across from him at the table. He asked me to hand him my ID papers, which I did. "How long have you been away from home?" he asked.

I did a quick calculation. "Since the start of my studies three years ago," I answered honestly.

"And what did you do the entire time in Egypt?"

"I've been taking classes, and…." My eyes fell on the baby on my lap and the two others the officers held.

"Are you married to an Egyptian?"

"Yes." He made a notation on his laptop.

"Why have you come back?"

"I want to visit my parents."

"Their names and address, please." He handed me a pen, and I jotted down the names of my father and my aunt, their address in Qarqan, and their cell numbers. A feeling of dread began to

creep over me. Should I have given out their personal information? I didn't want to cause them any trouble. On the other hand,
I couldn't supply false information, either.

"Do your parents know that you're coming?"

"Of course." He made another note.

"And how long do you plan to stay with them?"

"One month."

"What exactly will you be doing during this time in Xinjiang?"

"Nothing special." What a dumb question, I thought. How in
the world was I supposed to do anything special when I had three
infants to care for? "I will simply be visiting my family."

He nodded. "Did you join a terrorist organization while in
Egypt?" he suddenly asked.

I stared at him. Was he being serious? "Of course not."

"But you're Muslim?"

As an Uyghur, he had to know that we were all Muslim by faith.
"Yes," I replied.

"Did you wear a headscarf while in Egypt?"

Another of these questions! At the moment, I wasn't wearing a
head covering because it was more practical for traveling and because
I hadn't wanted any religious garb to attract undue attention upon
my arrival in China. However, I had frequently worn a headscarf in
Egypt for various reasons. On the one hand, I knew that it pleased
Mahmud. On the other hand, it was safer for a woman to keep her
head covered in the volatile political environment that had recently
arisen there. Would I arouse the officer's mistrust if I admitted that?

"Sometimes I did," I replied.

He asked a few more questions. After that, Mohammed, on my
lap, as well as the other two babies, gradually grew restless. I believe they sensed the uneasy atmosphere in the room.

"Well, that's enough," the officer finally said.

He stood up. I was about to do the same, expecting that I would
be allowed to continue on my journey now, but at that moment,

another officer stepped toward me and demanded that I hand Mohammed to her.

"What for?"

"Don't ask so many questions," she said, holding her arms out to take the baby.

I instinctively turned my body, knowing I couldn't let her take him away. However, the officer had already grabbed hold of him and tore him out of my arms. Mohammed started to sob, and the two other children, whom the two plainclothes officers were still holding, began shrieking.

Suddenly I realized that something terrible was happening. "Hand my children back to me right now!" I shouted, but the officers didn't respond. Instead, hands grabbed me tightly, and I screamed my head off.

I will never forget that moment as long as I live, the moment they ripped my oldest son out of my arms and I couldn't get to him. Even today, I can still hear his cries, and even today, I can still see Mohammed's terrified eyes in my nightmares. Night after night, this image haunts me.

The officers grabbed me by the arms and instantly snapped handcuffs around my wrists. Someone put a gag in my mouth. "Lean over!" shouted the man who had interrogated me. Everything happened in a flash. Someone behind me yanked a black sack over my head, and everything around me fell into darkness. They then dragged me out of the room.

I stumbled blindly in the direction that the officers were shoving and yanking me by the hands. They continued to bark orders at me: "Now turn right, now lift your feet," they said. "We're at a step. Up you go!"

I was eventually pushed roughly into a vehicle, at which point I bumped my face against something hard. A sharp pain shot through my body. I had rammed my nose into the doorframe, and it was bleeding profusely. I felt the blood gush down my face, and I cried out. "Stop that!" a man's voice shouted. "I told you to lift your feet."

A door slammed shut behind me, and I heard an engine turn over. The van, with me in the back, lurched forward. Someone fumbled around with my nose, obviously trying to staunch the blood with a cloth, though with little success. He finally removed my sack and wiped my face off with the cloth. It was an Uyghur officer who was guarding me.

All told, there were four officers in the van with me: three Uyghurs and one Chinese man. The Chinese man was wearing a different uniform and was the only one carrying a pistol and a baton on his belt. Obviously, he was the commanding officer over the others, each of whom was guarding a prisoner. Besides myself, two additional individuals were transported with sacks over their heads.

They didn't remove the sacks from the other two, and none of us spoke. I couldn't tell what our destination was because the back of the van only had one small, highly-placed window. Nonetheless, I could see that it was dark outside; occasionally, I caught the flash of headlights, but nothing more.

We drove along for about half an hour, then the road lighting outside grew brighter; we had apparently reached the downtown area of Ürümqi. We passed a boom gate and drove into a courtyard area. Since my guard had left my sack off for the rest of the trip, I was able to see that we had pulled into a police station yard. It reminded me of the station where one of my uncles worked, who was also a police officer.

The officers ordered us to get out and guided us into the building, where we entered a stairwell that was brightly illuminated by cold neon light. I was led into the cellar with an officer in front of me and another at my back. We descended to the floor below this, then to the second, and finally down one more staircase to the third. I would never have thought that this building reached so far underground.

Way down there, we entered a corridor flanked by metal bars behind which were crowded people of all nationalities, often up to a dozen in a single cell. I saw all sorts of Asian women, mostly composed of individuals from Muslim nations such as Pakistan or Indonesia. However, a few blue-eyed Europeans and even Americans were scattered among them. A strong stench emanated from them. They watched the arrival of us three newcomers with a mixture of disgust, helplessness, and despair. I wondered why in the world I had been brought to this place. Did the officers mistakenly think that I was a foreigner, too? I found myself hoping that perhaps all of this would reveal itself to be the result of some terrible mix-up.

I was locked in a cell with two women, a young Indonesian and a Malaysian. The two of them looked extremely haggard and had frightened eyes. The Malaysian woman, wearing a colorful headscarf, was very petite and had small eyes, like the Chinese. The Indonesian was somewhat plumper; she had chocolate-colored skin and wore a dirty, white hijab. Both women had been in custody for a long time, but just like me, they were still handcuffed. An argument broke out between the officers who had accompanied me about whether the foreigners or I, the Uyghur, were supposed to be interrogated first. They eventually decided on the foreigners and took the Indonesian off with them first.

In the meantime, I sat down in the cell and waited. What would the officers do with me, I wondered. Then, perhaps, when my turn to be interrogated came, I could finally clear up the misunderstanding that had led to my arrest. I had to get back to my babies, after all. My sore breasts reminded me they were bound to be hungry, and it broke my heart that I couldn't nurse them. Where were they right now? And who was consoling them when they cried?

Suddenly one of the offers appeared in front of the bars and asked me if I spoke English. I said that I could. "Then you're going to interpret for us," he declared.

He led me to a brightly lit room without any windows. There was only one dark pane of glass, behind which another room was concealed. The Indonesian woman was sitting across from several officers at a table in the center of the room; two officers were wearing Uyghur uniforms. The third man had the smooth hair and flat features of the Chinese. He sat between the two other men and led the interrogation. When I was brought inside, he only glanced at me briefly before gesturing for me to sit down next to the Indonesian woman.

The woman's face was now covered with red spots. She attempted to explain that she was studying in Ürümqi and had gone home to visit her parents during her semester break. However, she could hardly express herself. "How can it be that, after one year of studying here, you still haven't mastered our language?" the lead interrogator asked aggressively. "And more importantly, why are you studying in Xinjiang and not in interior China?"

He ordered me to translate his words into English, which I did. However, the woman looked just as perplexed as before. And so, I tried once more in Arabic. This she understood. "I wanted to study in China, and I was very glad when the university in Ürümqi accepted me," she replied.

The interrogator narrowed his eyes to thin slits as he glanced back and forth between the two of us suspiciously. "Hey, which language was that?" he asked. "Were you speaking Arabic?"

I confirmed this, but it would have been better if I hadn't. Instead, the interrogation now focused exclusively on why the two of us spoke such good Arabic. I talked about my time studying in Egypt; the other woman explained that, as a child, she had attended a Koran school. And just like that, all the warning alarms went off in the officers. "Are you an agent? Are you trying to return Chinese state secrets to Indonesia?" they asked accusingly.

"I don't understand what you mean. I don't want to work here; only study," the girl stammered.

Only after what felt like an eternity did they break off the interrogation with the Indonesian and lead in the Malaysian. As I found out, there was also a language problem with her.

She had been arrested because someone had discovered a key setting in her computer that allowed her to use Arabic characters. The woman lived in Malaysia but was visiting Xinjiang since she was married to an Uyghur man. She tried carefully to explain to the officers that in her homeland, it was completely normal to have Arabic character options on computers since the Malay language was originally written in Jawi script, which was based on the Arabic language.

"But the Latin alphabet had replaced it," the interrogator cut in.

"Nonetheless, you still sometimes need Arabic characters," the woman declared.

"You need them for religious texts! Admit it!" the Chinese man shouted.

The woman denied everything, refusing to declare that her key settings had anything to do with religious motivations. Instead, she demanded to be allowed to contact her consulate. The officers seemed to get a tickle out of this, grinning broadly. "Do you know how many people here have asked to contact their consulates?" one of the Uyghurs inquired. "You can forget that. We're your consulate now!"

They yanked off the woman's headscarf and dropped it on the floor. She leaned down and tried to put it back on, which was challenging since her hands were still shackled. The officers chuckled as they watched her. They patiently waited until she had the scarf back on, and then one of them stepped over to tear it back off again. And so she bent down once more.

This continued for a while, during which the woman grew increasingly frantic as the officers became more and more gleeful at her dismay. The entire scene was an exercise in humiliation. However, the officers obviously felt challenged by her resistance, as reflected in their increasing aggression. They eventually started to punch her in the face as she busied herself with her scarf.

Exhausted and scared, the woman broke into tears. "I need to see my child," she sobbed. "Do you have no pity whatsoever for a mother?" I learned that, like me, she had a newborn from which she had already been separated for a week. "Do what you want to me, but let me nurse my baby!" she begged.

"Not until you cooperate and give us all the information we want," the interrogator replied unrelentingly.

I was shocked by these two interrogations. As I now realize, the officers had no qualms regarding leveraging our children against us. I knew they would attempt the same tactic with me, and I might not see my three babies for a long time.

Back in the cell, I fell into a comatose sleep caused by my utter exhaustion. Since our departure from Egypt, I had been awake for almost forty-eight hours straight. No wonder, despite the fearful environment and the hard floor, my eyes fell shut as I sat there. I might have slept for an hour or a few minutes. In the midst of my deep sleep, I was awakened by a guard who materialized in front of me and shook me out of my sleep. "Come with me!" he yelled.

He led me to the interrogation room that I had been in before. However, this time I found different interrogators waiting there. I sat across from a new team of Chinese and Uyghur officers. The officer in charge was a middle-aged Chinese man with the same emotionless gaze and cold eyes as his predecessor. A stack of documents sat in front of him. An Uyghur policeman with angry furrows carved deeply across his forehead sat next to him.

While the Chinese man initially ignored me as he stared at his papers, the Uyghur ordered the guard to tie me to my chair. "That way, you won't get too comfortable with us," he said.

I think he did this to intimidate me, but I had already decided I wouldn't let them antagonize or faze me in any way. On the contrary: I would behave with absolute cooperation. Then, when the officers realized that I wasn't keeping any secrets from them, they would perhaps see their error–and release me. That was the vague hope to which I was clinging.

The Chinese officer opened the conversation by reading my name and date of birth aloud. He then wanted to verify that what he had on record about my birthplace and my father's address were correct. I confirmed for him the information I had already provided at the airport. I assumed he wanted to be assured that I had told the truth from the beginning.

The Chinese man also asked for the names of my two half-siblings. "Where is your sister studying?" he asked.

I hesitated briefly. Did I have the right to drag her into all this? I wondered as my resolution to be fully cooperative momentarily wavered. However, I told myself that he could easily get this information through other channels and that he would be favorably inclined toward me if I willingly offered it to him. And so, I gave him the name of her university.

"And your brother lives with your parents?"

It sounded as if he already knew this. I was about to ask him how he knew that, but I ordered myself to stay focused on his questions. "Yes, that's right," I replied.

He then went through my resume with me. I had to give him the name of the school in Toraklik and any other schools and the college I had attended in Guangzhou. He asked for the names of my teachers and fellow students and wanted specific details about the part-time jobs I had worked during my student years.

He eventually asked me why I had gone to Cairo. I explained to him that I had wanted to study there. "But why not in China?" he pressed. "Wouldn't that have been easier? Or do you not trust the Chinese educational system?"

"Of course I do. But studying abroad appealed to me."

"Ah. And why was that?"

"I'm interested in foreign languages. Besides, I thought the international experience would increase my job opportunities."

"Okay, but why Egypt, of all places? Why a Muslim country?"

"It was what I could afford, and...."

"Yes?"

Should I be honest? If so, I would have to admit that Arabic–a language in which I had some basic proficiency–is spoken in Egypt also influenced my decision to include the country on my short list of potential nations in which to study. However, I could still envision my Indonesian cellmate, who had confessed under interrogation that she had learned Arabic at a Koran school.

Something similar was also true for me. Even before going to Egypt, I had been interested in Arabic since it was the language in which our holy book, the Koran, had been written. But I didn't want to make the same mistake the Indonesian woman made, so I remained silent.

"Do you think we don't already know that even during your school years, you were eager to live among Muslims?" the Chinese man asked.

"That isn't true."

"Really? Then why did you persuade your schoolmates to adopt the Islamic faith? And why did you marry an Arab man?"

I was speechless in the face of how much he knew about me–and how cleverly he worked with insinuations. "It was... love," I stammered. "We fell in love."

He laughed loudly. "How sweet," he said. "Truly."

The Chinese officer fumbled for a package of cigarettes in his chest pocket and lit one. He exhaled the smoke appreciatively before urging the Uyghur to help himself to one as well. And so they just sat there across from me and puffed away as smoke slowly spread throughout the windowless room. I started to cough and asked if I could have a glass of water. My throat was terribly dry.

"Do you have any other wishes? Are we in a luxury hotel here?" the Uyghur officer snapped at me as he blew smoke into my face.

The interview lasted for hours, focusing primarily on my time in Cairo. The two officers had me explain in detail what my life had been like there. They inquired what cafes I had frequented, which mosques in the city I had visited, and who my friends had been, both inside and outside the university. They diligently wrote down all the names I gave them. I realized at some point that someone was listening in on us from the other side of the dark pane of glass. I couldn't see his face, just the outline of his head and torso. He stood up eventually and walked into our room. Another Chinese policeman then took over the interrogation along with a different Uyghur man.

And so the officers changed places from time to time. The replacements were always wide awake and well-informed about the ground we had already covered. On the other hand, I grew increasingly tired.

I lost all track of time, but I felt my interrogation stretched over several days.

I would reach the point that I didn't think I could bear the garish light a moment longer, and my eyes literally closed. Whenever that happened, someone immediately began to shake me awake or would slap me on the back of the head. "Hey, we aren't done here yet!" they warned me. They refused to give me even one second of peace.

Time and again, I had to answer the same questions. "Why did you go abroad? Why did you marry an Arab man? Why are you wearing a headscarf? Are you a member of a terrorist organization?" Finally, I couldn't stand it a minute longer.

"No. I already told you! I'm not a terrorist!" I shouted at them.

"How many Uyghurs did you know in Cairo?" they continued, unperturbed.

"I have no idea! Maybe a dozen?" I have to pull myself together, I told myself. Fatigue was making me lose my composure, and that was dangerous. But this was obviously their goal.

I tried to marshal my mental faculties and concentrate on what was happening. But I was slowly losing hope that this interrogation would never end. In addition, I developed a painful headache because the air quality in the room was so poor; I also felt an almost superhuman thirst.

When I finally reached the end of my strength, they waved several photos under my nose, showing various Uyghur men and women who lived in Cairo as I had. The interrogator went through them, one at a time, with me. As he came to each image, he asked me if I knew the person, and if I said yes, he demanded that I give them their names and any details I knew about their lives in Cairo. "What is she studying?" he asked one of my classmates. "Does she go to the mosque every Friday? Does she wear a headscarf when she does?"

In the face of these questions, I felt nauseous but forced myself to remember my resolve to stay cooperative. Nonetheless, this was where I hit my limits: I couldn't inform on my friends and acquaintances!

And with that, I fell silent. The officers did the same. "We have lots of time," the Chinese man declared as he blew smoke in my direction.

"Your poor babies," the Uyghur officer remarked. "Can you hear them crying close by?"

I listened. Despite my declining mental state, I was aware that he was probably trying to rattle me. Nonetheless, for one long moment, I thought I could hear my babies crying down here in the cellar. The officer noticed the alert tension on my face. "There, do you hear them?" he asked.

At that moment, I snapped. "You're all monsters!" I bellowed. "Give me my children right now! I have to nurse them, or they'll starve!"

"Well, well," the Uyghur man said. "Now, who's getting impatient?"

"We're already taking care of your children," the Chinese officer interjected, a cold smile on his lips.

At that, the last remnant of my self-control fell apart. I sobbed in anger and despair, but the two men continued mercilessly. "One more time: What is the woman studying?" The Chinese man repeated the question I had refused to answer before. "Don't deny that you know her."

But I was no longer an in any condition to answer him. I couldn't think about anything but my children. I sat across from the two officers and wept. The Chinese man angrily slammed his fist down on the table.

"Cut that out!" he yelled. "You're unwilling to help us. And you refuse to confess your crimes."

"What crimes?" I sniffed. "What am I supposed to confess? I haven't...."

"See what I mean!" he interrupted me harshly. "We'll need to punish you more severely to help your memory start working again."

Two Uyghur guards untied me from the chair. At first, I was relieved that I was being released from my uncomfortable position. Every limb in my body ached because the interrogation had lasted for a total of three days. I expected them to take me back to the cell with the Malaysian and the Indonesian women, but that wasn't what they did. Instead, the men positioned me between them and conducted me down a long corridor, at the end of which was a door leading to a dark antechamber. Another door was located at the back of this space, and behind that was my new cell.

The chamber they now locked me in was cramped and pitch black. It was so dark that you couldn't see your hand in front of your eyes. A red dot in the corner was the only tiny spark of light in the dark void. It was presumably from a camera that was mounted to the wall. Otherwise, there was nothing in here: no light, sound, furnishings, and, most importantly, no other human soul. Completely alone, I crouched there on the cool stone floor between the oppressively narrow walls.

I was able to bear it for the first few hours. After the interrogation, I initially crumpled wearily on the floor and slept for quite a while. I have no idea how long that was, but when I woke up, it was still dark. And I was still alone. I listened to the silence and waited for something to happen. But nothing occurred. Nothing happened for hours and hours, and I slowly began to suspect what was still in store for me.

In my mind, I played back the scenes that had taken place since my arrival in China. I couldn't comprehend all of it: How had I landed in this horrific yet absurd situation? How could I have let the officers take my children away from me? What would Mahmud say about this? He had arrived back in Cairo by now and was bound to wonder why he wasn't hearing anything from me. And nobody would inform him about what was going on with us.

I went back through the long interrogation and wondered if there was anything I should have done differently. I still couldn't understand what the police accused me of–and what they wanted me to confess to. Was the crime my being a Muslim? Should I have possibly denied that in order to seem less suspicious? On the other hand, they would have inevitably proved that I was lying. After all, Uyghurs were Muslim by faith, and there were also photos of me wearing a headscarf. They even showed me some of those.

The Chinese authorities had been closely watching not only me but all of the Uyghurs in Cairo. They must have spied on us, watched us as we visited mosques, photographed us whenever we met in cafes, and tracked our social media accounts. As a result, the people here knew exactly who were friends with whom, who worked where, and what each of us earned. Although we lived far away from Xinjiang and China, they maintained surveillance at every moment of our lives.

It was astonishing in its own right, but what was behind it? I couldn't understand why they would have gone to such expense. Did they think that all women who wore headscarves were terrorists? If that was the case, I was in trouble. "Allah, give them insight into the truth," I begged God.

However, I was mainly tormented by thoughts about my children. I was horribly scared for my three babies, who were completely defenseless in the face of the Chinese authorities' caprice. Where were the three of them located at the moment? Were they doing alright? Were they being given formula? I could hear them screaming in my head because they were hungry and wanted to nurse. Oh, I so longed for their tiny, greedy mouths!

I started to make terrible self-accusations. Why had I even brought the three of them along on this trip? It hadn't been necessary! All five of us could have stayed back in Cairo. None of this would have happened if I hadn't insisted on introducing them to my parents. This made it all my fault—mine and mine alone.

I racked my brain for answers. The longer I wound myself up in my thoughts, the more they tortured me. In my tiny, dark cell, there was no escape from them. Before long, my thoughts circled around one and only one image: my children, my children, my children. What kind of mother was I if I hadn't been able to keep them safe? In the darkness, I saw their beloved, gentle faces and heard them scream heartbreakingly for me, louder and louder.

That was worse than any torture. I practically yearned to be back in the room with the officers who had interrogated me. At least there, I had been distracted. But now my mind had nothing to do except construct my mental hell. A hell that I had to endure without any respite. Then again, perhaps this was my just punishment. I was to blame for whichever way I twisted and turned it. I was to blame. I was to blame.

The only interruption to the dark monotony of my thoughts was when food was shoved into my cell through the slit in the door.

But even then, I didn't interact with anyone; nobody spoke to me. The only thing I heard was the sound made against the stone floor by the metal dish holding a small serving of porridge or soup. I sometimes consumed a little of this if I felt hungry. But most of the time, I couldn't keep the food down. In one of the corners of the room, there was a hole in the floor. This was the toilet, and that was where I scraped my vomit.

In my total isolation, I almost went insane. I felt as if I had been buried alive. Was I even still alive? Everything grew blurry in my mind.

I no longer had any sense of how much time had passed. Had I been here for several days, weeks, or even a year? Did anyone out there still miss me? In my desperation, I even began to think that I could hold a conversation with the camera. "If a human being is sitting on the other side, please have mercy on me!" I pleaded. "I have three small children who are crying for me incessantly." Another time, I sang a lullaby for my babies.

But I never received an answer. There was only darkness and silence.

CHAPTER 5

Trapped in Hell

"Hey, get her out. The week is up!" After a long time in my prison, I finally heard a human voice... and was astonished. Only seven days? It felt as if I had spent seven centuries in that dark space.

A key rattled in the door as an Uyghur guard spoke with his colleague. My heart pounding, I watched the door open a crack, and the two men stepped inside. The light that flooded the room from the hallways blinded me, but not for long. One of the men moved close to me and pulled another dark sack over my head. "Come with me," he said.

Somewhat clumsily, I followed them out. I could hardly believe it: They were freeing me! I was finally allowed to leave the dark hell of these four walls!

Exhausted and uncertain, I trailed them down the corridor to the stairwell, where they ordered me to lift my feet to climb the stairs. My muscles protested loudly after such a long period of inactivity, but I ordered myself to tense them. After all, I wanted nothing more than to escape this abysmal cellar. I would finally see the light of day again!

They led me up all three flights to the ground floor, by which point I was breathing heavily, and took me into a room where a female guard took off my clothing. She removed the cardigan, pair of jeans, and stinking t-shirt I had worn the entire time. She then pulled on a fresh pair of pants and ordered me to raise my arms so she could put a fresh shirt on me.

When she finished, she returned me to the two male guards. "Now down here to the left and then right," they ordered me. I heard a door being unlocked. Were they finally going to release me? They shoved me across a threshold – into freedom? I registered whispering voices as the foul stench of sweat washed over me. "There you go," one of the guards said as he removed the sack from my head.

I blinked. Where was I? My eyes had grown so accustomed to the darkness that I couldn't make anything out at first. The sudden brightness was painful, but then I became aware of the numerous women standing around me, about thirty of them, pressed tightly against each other and eying me curiously. They were Uyghur women, or, more precisely, Uyghur prisoners, as I could tell from the fact that they were all wearing identical blue uniforms. I looked down at myself and was shocked to see I was wearing the same outfit. I now found myself in a prison cell. It was about forty square meters and had no windows. However, there were two ventilation holes on the sides and an opening in the ceiling through which daylight streamed.

I was incredibly disappointed when I realized that I wasn't being released – and that there was no indication that that would happen at any time in the foreseeable future. "Why aren't you letting me go?" I shouted after my guards, who had already left the cell and locked the door from the outside. "I haven't done anything!" They didn't respond. "I'm innocent!" But they were already gone, and I was stuck alone with the other women.

I wanted to sob. Robbed of every hope of a quick or happy ending to my odyssey, I dropped to the floor. "Stop it," a woman whispered, hardly audible. "You'll just attract trouble."

I didn't know what she meant, but I followed her gaze and discovered the camera mounted in the corner of the room. She nodded imperceptibly. Yes, they're watching us. The woman's eyes darted around to the other corners, and sure enough, there were cameras all over the cell, tracking us and recording our every movement.

The woman was quite pretty, despite her blue prison uniform. There was something rather noble about her; her skin was fair, and she gazed at me out of remarkably large eyes. How had such an elegant woman ended up here, I wondered.

"What's your name?" I asked.

"Ilham," she replied tersely.

"Have you been here long?"

"Two months."

I was shocked. Two months! In other words, practically forever. I wanted to ask her questions, but she silently indicated that I should hold my tongue. I understood why shortly after that. "Silence! Prisoner Number 24, this is your first warning!" a woman's voice bellowed out of a loudspeaker. She was obviously speaking to me. I gathered from the announcement that I had been assigned the number 24. A glance at the badge on the left side of my prison shirt confirmed this assumption. There was my last name and the number 24.

I gradually realized that strict governance held sway in my cell. We weren't allowed to speak with each other. Nor were we permitted to move around in there as we wished. We had to ask permission before we could do anything, and we did this through an intercom system. That was the only way we could communicate with the officers who were monitoring us the whole time via the cameras. To do that, we had to wave at the cameras and wait until they called on us.

We even had to ask permission for mundane things like going to the bathroom. A hole in the floor was located in the corner of the cell, and we had to relieve ourselves there in front of everyone, although only after we had asked for permission to do that. And it wasn't as if we could go to the bathroom whenever we liked. They would refuse to consent if we asked too often – or if our watchers on the other side of the wall were having a bad day. It was very uncomfortable, and sometimes the women in question wet themselves.

Besides that, the speaker system functioned as a means to bark out warnings and give us orders. This started around 4:30 every morning when they woke us up with a deafeningly loud announcement and ordered us to get up on our feet. Next, they told us to line up like soldiers; each of us had assigned spots to stand in. And once we were all standing in an orderly fashion, we were commanded to march in place without moving forward a single step. As we did this, we had to sing the national anthem, the so-called March of the Volunteers, which wasn't without a certain degree of irony considering the lyrics:

Stand up! All who refuse to be slaves anymore!
With our flesh and blood,
Let us build the new walls.
The Chinese people are in their greatest distress.
The final cry of the oppressed sounds:
Stand up! Rise up!
Together against enemy fire, onward!
Together against enemy fire, onward!
Onward! Onward! Onward!

We spent at least half an hour every morning singing and marching, sometimes even longer than that. As we did this, we repeated the anthem countless times. At some point, our heads were filled to the brim with the melody and the lyrics. You could hear nothing except the anthem and could think of hardly anything else. In a way, this was a relief. At least, I found it to be so.

After the morning march, the toilet visits began. These consumed a lot of time because only one woman at a time could use the latrine. Afterward, the cell stank barbarically. In my early days in the cell, I was so ashamed to go in front of the others that I actually couldn't relieve myself. However, I eventually got a terrible stomachache and had nothing to do but imitate my cellmates' actions.

For "breakfast," all we received was a cup of rice water. To get one of these, we had to form a line at the door, and each woman had to step up singly to the guards, her head bowed. This was because the guards claimed that good ideas could only flow into a person's mind if she bowed her head. In other words, the ideology of the Communist Party of China. "If you accept that you are in the wrong, we won't be so hard on you," they said. "But if you refuse to admit this, we will make things very difficult for you."

We also had to repeat sentences that were dictated to us actively. The guards, mainly young men from distant provinces, recited the slogans to us, and we had to repeat them. However, they often spoke so quickly that the Uyghur women had difficulty understanding them. Many women, thus, parroted the Chinese words and tried to make no mistakes because they would otherwise feel the effects of the men's electric stun batons. I also bowed my head and said: "I admit I'm in the wrong." I wouldn't have been given any rice water if I hadn't. Unlike many others, though, I understood the meaning of the words very well, and they disgusted me.

The rice water tasted terrible. Quite a few women vomited after consuming it because it upset their stomachs. Nonetheless, I drank it greedily since I desperately needed the liquid. Now that May had arrived, it was getting hotter with each passing day, and I sweated profusely as the temperature in our cell rose. Besides the rice water, we only received a single cup of water during the day.

After the morning routine, the guards brought the "Red Book" into our cell. We received ten copies of this volume, which were carefully counted and numbered so that none of them could vanish. This book – not to be confused with Mao Tse-tung's *Little Red Book* – is something of a state secret in China. It only exists in prisons, camps, and police academies – in other words, anywhere where people are supposed to be indoctrinated. The book contains the slogans of the Communist Party, in addition to quotes from Mao and General Secretary Xi Jinping, and patriotic song lyrics. While in prison, these texts became the content of our lives.

We had to memorize the entire book, word for word, every day a different passage. They instructed us over the loudspeaker on how exactly we should proceed. One morning, for example, they told us to crouch on the floor and read a particular page. Many women hadn't attended a Chinese university as I had, and they were completely overwhelmed. They couldn't decipher even a single one of the characters. "I can't make out any of the words," confessed the woman with the large eyes who had introduced herself as Ilham the day I had arrived.

"Should I help you?"

She nodded imperceptibly, and I slid a little closer. I quietly began to read the texts on the page to her and to explain their meaning. The other women sitting near us also listened because they faced the same problem. They had to be able to recite the texts later; otherwise, they ran the risk of losing their meals or being beaten. At first, I was nervous, but then I relaxed. The officers behind the cameras, who were watching our activities, seemed to accept my tutoring assistance silently. In any case, I didn't receive another warning over the loudspeaker. After one's third warning, the guards typically punished you with a beating, but I was fortunately spared that fate.

PLACE OF NO RETURN

"Thank you," Ilham murmured later.

"You're welcome," I whispered. And then we had to stop talking again to keep from attracting attention to ourselves.

The loudspeaker then announced our next activity: We had to stand up and turn our heads alternately to the right and the left. As we did this, we were supposed to recite the texts we had just read. "The Revolution and the recognition of classes and class conflict are necessary for the Chinese people to defeat its internal and external enemies." We repeated in unison this saying from Mao Tse-tung. Ilham winked at me conspiratorially since she could also recite this quote accurately.

Besides the revolutionary leader Mao, General Secretary Xi Jinping was among the most quoted individuals in the book. The authors always labeled him as our "Great Leader." "It is our responsibility to toil hard for the renewal of the Chinese nation," we had to memorize.

After half an hour, we changed our activity once more. The loudspeaker voice now demanded that we march in place as we sang Communist songs, which were also printed in the book. It went on for the entire day. The order of things fluctuated, but the same activities repeated themselves over and over again. We read texts out of the book, sang propaganda songs, or spouted Communist slogans we had learned by heart beforehand. We marched, exercised, or sat still, depending on what the voice on the loudspeaker declared. First and foremost, we weren't allowed even one minute, from early to late, to devote ourselves or our thoughts.

The fixed points in our daily routine were the "meal" times – these were both the zeniths and the nadirs, so to speak. Every noontime, we formed a line at the door once more to get a piece of steamed bun. Since we hadn't consumed anything except rice water since early morning, our stomachs were always growling by this point – and the guards knew that. This was why they liked to play little games with us so much.

Sometimes they insulted and humiliated us. For example, when we approached the door, they would say, "You're all criminals. The Communist Party is very generous to feed you anyway." Or they would tie the distribution of the rations to certain conditions. They usually demanded that I sing the national anthem for them. Only after that would they give me my mantou.

People typically eat these steamed yeast buns right out of the oven, but the bread they gave us was already days old and as hard as a rock. So all you could do was suck on the buns because you couldn't chew them into small pieces.

Our afternoons were filled with more political indoctrination and militaristic exercises. Occasionally, there were also special tasks, such as the command to clean our cell. For that, we were each given a tiny towel but no water. We had to clean the room down to the farthest corner. We crawled around on our hands and knees to accomplish that.

In the evenings, the guards organized the degrading procedure of food distribution for a third time. This time, if we were lucky, we received a bowl of cooked rice and another steamed bun. Some of us were beaten as we claimed our food, while others who couldn't perform the tasks demanded of us or spoke Chinese poorly walked away empty-handed and had to dream about the next morning.

Around 10 pm, they finally left us in peace, and the overhead lights were turned off. However, we couldn't stretch out on the floor to sleep; there wasn't enough space to accommodate so many of us. Only about one-third of the women got to enjoy the privilege of being able to stretch out completely. Everyone else had to try to sleep sitting up. Back to back, we sat in the hot cell and waited until our eyes fell shut in exhaustion. We changed positions in the middle of the night, and another group of women could lie down for a while.

I suffered a lot during these nights. The heat and the strong smell emanating from the numerous bodies around me were almost more than I could bear. Why I wondered, did I have to be so unnaturally close to all these strangers all the time? Above all, however, I was tormented by the thought of my children. I thought about them constantly and wondered where they were now. In some state facility? What wouldn't I have done to cradle them in my arms just for a moment or to caress their small, gentle faces?

I was also suffering physically. Hardly two months had passed since my C-section, and my body still wasn't properly healed. Besides that, my breasts ached because they were still producing milk. Since nobody was nursing from them, they often swelled up so much in those early days that I thought I would explode. I sometimes woke up at night only to realize my clothes were soaked with breast milk.

I was squeezed between two women – and I could do nothing except sit still. Weeping silently, I would wait for my clothes to dry, for tomorrow to come, and for another day in hell to begin. There was no point in waiting or hoping for anything. I was stuck here, parted from my children for half an eternity already, and I was losing every bit of faith I had in ever seeing them again. My stubborn body was the only thing that didn't want to accept this.

"What's wrong?" I heard a quiet voice whisper in the darkness. It belonged to Ilham, who was leaning against my back. Even though I was trying hard not to make any sound, because of the cameras, she had probably noticed the trembling of my body.

"Nothing," I whispered back, just as quietly.

"Just tell me," she insisted. "Why are you crying?"

"I'm... leaking milk." Another shudder ran through me, and I could hardly continue. "Milk for my children."

"What children?"

Ilham didn't seem to understand. "I have three newborns," I explained to her. "Triplets. And my breasts are constantly producing milk for them. If I make too much, it just runs out."

"Really?!" She sounded both astonished and shocked at the same time. "How old are they?"

"Two months."

"My God! You must miss them terribly!"

I sniffled quietly, though still too loudly. "Silence, Number 24!" ordered the loudspeaker. "This is your second warning!"

We instantly fell silent since we both knew that after the third warning, the beatings would start. Nonetheless, I found it comforting that Ilham was interested in my story and that she was brave enough to talk to me. The gesture counted a lot in this inhumane environment.

After our nighttime encounter, she and I made use of every opportunity to exchange a few words, naturally only in all secrecy. We acted like forbidden lovers who inconspicuously sought each other's proximity but were painstakingly careful that no one noticed.

I learned that she hadn't had any children yet. "I got married not too long ago," she whispered as we bent over the Red Book, acting as if we were engrossed in the lesson.

"How long ago was that?"

"Six months."

"Is he a good man?"

She blushed. "Yes, very…"

I was about to ask where her husband was now and how she was coping with the separation, but then the loudspeaker crackled to life, and some officer ordered us to start marching in place.

Right after that, Ilham was suddenly taken away by the guards. They called out her number and ordered her to go with them. I can still see the frightened glance she shot me, which was the last I saw of her for a while. By the end of the second day of her absence, I wondered if perhaps she had been released. Maybe she had been reunited with the husband she loved so much. I wished that for her. But that same evening, shortly after supper had been distributed, she was shoved back into our cell.

Ilham looked horrible. She had dark rings under her eyes and bruises across her face. I knew what that meant. "Did they interrogate you?" I murmured to her as we stood in a blind spot between two cameras. She confirmed my suspicion.

"It was because of my husband," she whispered. "He's Iranian, and we lived together in Dubai." The officers were convinced she must have been in contact with radical Muslims there and demanded that she confess this to them. It reminded me a lot of my own story. "If only I hadn't decided to visit my parents in Ürümqi," Ilham remarked quietly. "I've brought trouble down on all of us."

I knew what Ilham meant. I also blamed myself over and over again for not staying in Egypt. All of us would have been spared so much if we had, especially my three children. Perhaps my parents would have been, too. If Ilham's reports were trustworthy, our relatives were being harassed in their homes. "Anyone who has a relative in prison also falls under suspicion," she explained.

"Under suspicion of having done what exactly?"

She shrugged. Our "crimes" remained a mystery to us.

CHAPTER 6

What Did You Do To My Son?

One morning in July, two officers appeared in our cell again shortly after we had drunk our rice water. The two of them were carrying the infamous batons on their belts. "Number 24, come forward!" they shouted. That was me. Had I done something wrong? Was I about to be punished? Maybe I was now in trouble for all the short little conversations I'd had with Ilham. Anxious and frightened, I stepped toward the door of the cell. Without any explanation, they pulled a dark sack over my head.

They pushed me into the corridor. The door slammed behind me, followed by the rattle of the keys my fellow prisoners and I knew all too well. However, this time, I was standing on the other, on the right side of the door. Should I let myself feel new hope? Or should I steel myself against another interrogation and new hardships? Or maybe freedom, after all? "Come with us," they ordered.

They led me to a room where a female officer removed the sack and handcuffs before stripping off my stinking, blue prison uniform. In exchange, she handed me the jeans, t-shirt, and cardigan I had been wearing on the day of my arrest. I sniffed them; all the pieces of clothing were clean and smelled like some tangy detergent.

I then sat across from the officer and an Uyghur policeman in a guard room, where they informed me that I was being released from detention. It sounded so absurd that I couldn't grasp what they were telling me at first. "You mean I may go?" I asked cautiously.

"Yes, you may go," the policeman said. "But you need to know that you are on our blacklist. We will arrest you again if you make even one wrong move."

"We'll be watching you," the other officer added.

"And remember: You have a responsibility for yourself and your father. He has vouched for you."

"What does that mean?"

"That means that you will be under house arrest at his home. And if you make even one false step, you won't be the only one in trouble. He will be, too," the man clarified, staring at me with piercing eyes. "You wouldn't want your father to end up in prison because of you, would you?"

What a malevolent and vicious threat! I said nothing in reply.

"Good," he continued. "All that remains now are the formalities. Sign here that you have received all of your personal items back from us." He handed me a document on which my name was printed and a line for my signature. I hesitated. All I had on my body were my clothes. Where were the rest of my things?

"What about my passport?"

"Your passport, ID card, and children's passports will remain in our custody."

"Ah," I said. "And my cell phone?"

"We are keeping that as well and have blocked your number. Effective immediately, you are forbidden to use a cell phone anyway. Now sign this," he urged. "Or would you prefer to stay here?"

Should I protest? "For heaven's sake, no!" a voice inside my head screamed. And so I picked up the pen and signed – whatever.

"Well done," the policeman said.

"What about my children?" I asked. "Where are they? Can I see them?"

"Of course," the female officer replied. My heart pounded faster. "That is why we're releasing you. They are in the municipal hospital."

I looked at her in bewilderment, but she wasn't willing to provide an explanation. "Your father has been notified," was all she said. "Go to him now. He's waiting outside for you."

The two officers opened the door and accompanied me out as if I were a visitor. I was still suspicious of this unexpected turn that my day had taken. Over the past two months, I have gazed into the abyss of the human soul. I had learned not to believe in anything and distrust everyone. That is why I wondered if the two officers were playing some devious mind game with me. Would they prevent me from leaving at the last minute and lock me back up with the other women?

However, nothing like that happened. I cautiously stepped through the door, out into the warm, dry June air. The much-too-bright sun blinded me. With deliberate slowness, I approached the barrier; I didn't want to reveal my nervousness. However, the guards there made no move to try to stop me. They let me pass through, and I left the police station without glancing back even once.

And then I caught sight of my father. I was terribly shocked to see that his hair had turned completely gray. When I last saw him in Egypt, his thinning hair had still been dark. Now he looked like an old man with infinitely sad eyes. "Mihrigul," he said.

I dove into his arms and heard him sob. He held me tightly against him.

"I'm sorry, Papa. I should've listened to you," I said.

"Shh, shh," he replied.

"You were right; I should never have studied abroad. If I hadn't, none of this would've happened."

He shook his head. "Nonsense."

"I'm so sorry that I've brought such trouble down on you... You shouldn't have vouched for me!" I lined up one apology after the other because I felt incredibly guilty.

"Just calm down. It's all over now."

And yet, I wasn't sure if that was true. After all I'd just been through, I was steeling myself for the next catastrophe, and feeling optimistic was hard.

"Let's go to the hospital now and pick up the babies. Everything will be better then," my father repeated.

"Definitely! I can't wait," I agreed. I would finally get to see my children again.

My father called for a taxi on his phone. As we slowly glided past the high-rise facades of Ürümqi in the taxi, I couldn't stop thinking about my three children and wondering how they had been doing all this time. During my weeks in prison, I had hoped they might have been taken to my parents, who would have lovingly taken care of their grandchildren. However, my father had known just as little about where they were being kept as I had. That is why we now assume they had been in the care of state institutions the entire time. Hopefully, the three of them had remained healthy, I thought anxiously. Hopefully, there was no serious reason why we needed to pick them up from the hospital, not from a state-run nursery. They had still been nursing at the time of our separation. That was why I was worried about whether or not they had received enough milk during this time.

"Don't worry so much, Mihrigul. The genes in our family are strong," my father tried to cheer me up.

However, I could hear the nervousness in his voice. Neither of us knew what to expect. And the closer we drew to the hospital, the more unbearable the uncertainty grew. On the one hand, my heart pounded in anticipation of finally seeing Mohammed, Moez, and Elena again. But, on the other hand, I could hardly keep my agitation and concern for the three of them in check.

At the reception area, I gave my name and presented the ticket the police had given me. The nurse who received us at the desk was informed about the situation. "Ah, Ms. Tursun, the mother of the triplets," he said.

"How are the three of them?"

"Please follow me."

He led us down a long corridor to a waiting room in the pediatric ward, where other relatives sat on long plastic benches. He gestured for us to take a seat there. "Please wait here for a moment," he said. "I will get the children." With these words, he disappeared. I longed to follow him.

The next minutes felt like an eternity. I rocked restlessly back and forth on the bench next to my father. "Why is he taking so long?" I murmured to him. "Can't he find the babies?"

"Maybe they're having to take care of some formalities," my father said soothingly. I nodded. I had to pull myself together. After our two months of separation, I could also survive this short time.

The nurse finally appeared at the door, carrying a baby. My baby! My heart started to race. I jumped up right away and stumbled toward the two of them. "Moez, my little boy!" I called. "My sweet little boy!"

The nurse handed me the infant swaddled a white blanket. As I could tell at first glance, he looked quite pale and emaciated. The only other oddity was that his head was strangely enlarged; it looked like an inflated balloon. Nonetheless, an unbelievable feeling of happiness flooded me as I held my beloved youngest son in my arms. "Moez! My little Moez," I kept repeating.

"Where are the other two?" I heard my father ask.

However, a second nurse was already approaching with another baby. It was Elena! My dear daughter Elena. The nurse handed me this infant as I dropped back down on the bench. I could hardly contain my joy; I now had two of my children in my arms.

I covered them both with kisses. Elena was just as small and haggard as her brother. However, her head was the right size compared to the rest of her body. I thought the two of them must have suffered from the abrupt switch to formula and not received enough nourishment. They were both cross-eyed now, something they hadn't been before. And the color of their skin worried me as well; it looked as if they had never been out in the fresh air. "This will change," I promised my children. "Starting today, you have a mother who will care for you again!"

I exchanged looks with my father, who was benevolently watching my two babies and me. He also had tears of joy in his eyes. "And where is the third child?" he asked the nurse.

The man avoided his gaze. "I can't bring him to you," he said.

"Why not?"

"He's still... uh, undergoing treatment. ."

I sobered up all of a sudden. What did that mean? What was going on with my oldest son? "Is Mohammed sick?"

"He's in the ICU," the man stammered.

"I want to take him with me anyway!" This demand crossed my lips more or less automatically. After all that I had experienced, I only wanted one thing: to pack up my three children and never again be parted from them.

"I regret that this won't be possible. His condition isn't very stable."

"What's wrong with him?"

"He's suffering from... respiratory distress."

Something about the way the man was speaking bothered me. I sensed panic rising up within me. What was he hiding from me? "I have to see my boy!" I begged. "Please!"

It felt as if the nurse was under instructions to keep me from seeing my child, but my father and I kept talking to him nonstop. We emphasized that we had a right to know what had happened to the boy. Finally, my father demanded that the nurse immediately fetch a doctor who could tell us what was wrong with the baby and why we couldn't take him with us. But the nurse squirmed and trotted out every possible explanation as to why this wasn't doable. He finally agreed to show us the baby from a distance.

He led us to the glass door behind which the ICU was located, where about half a dozen young children were being treated. They were lying in small beds, most of which were outfitted with all kinds of apparatus and tubes. It looked downright creepy, and I felt my stomach clench. The man pointed to the farthest corner of the room. "There, way in the back is your boy," he declared, pointing at a baby who was on a ventilator. I pressed my face against the pane of glass. Was that my son? Of course, I saw a baby but couldn't recognize him.

"Let me see him for a moment," I begged again.

"No, you really can't," the nurse insisted. There were allegedly hygienic reasons why we couldn't be allowed to get closer to the bassinet. "Please go home now," he said. "Our visiting hours are over."

With heavy hearts, we left the hospital without Mohammed. Nonetheless, we still had the other two children, which consoled me. At least my two younger babies were now with me again – and I would return to the hospital by tomorrow at the latest and insist to the doctors that they give me my eldest as well.

We drove straight to the hotel where my father had rented a room. My aunt was there waiting for us. She looked incredulous when she saw my father and me at the door with the two children and hugged me enthusiastically. "My God, you're finally here!" she said, "and with the little ones, too! I had started to think you'd gotten lost."

My father went right back out to buy some powdered milk since I was no longer producing enough breast milk. In the meantime, Menzire and I started a major cleaning endeavor. My aunt first banished me to the bathroom, where I peeled off my clothes and got under the shower. Letting warm water run down my body felt like a great luxury. When I scrubbed myself with the soap, I watched as it turned brown, proofing that I was filthy.

Then we focused on the babies; we bathed Elena and Moez in the sink. I was once again struck by how thin they both were. I could touch each of Moez's ribs individually, and his breathing was quite shallow. I tenderly washed his small body and noticed that he wasn't just dirty but also had open sores in some spots. I assumed that he had been forced to lie in his crib for too long. I carefully examined the rest of his body and was shocked to discover a cut on his neck.

"Look, what is that?" I asked Menzire, who was standing beside me and caring for Elena. She gingerly traced the line across Moez's throat, and he instantly started to cry.

"How odd it looks," she said. "What could have happened?"

I had no idea, but I was also curious. I now examined Elena's throat and found a similar, elongated cut. Suddenly I felt very strange. "Do you see that?" I asked my aunt, pointing at the mark on Elena's neck. Just like Moez's wound, hers wasn't completely healed, either. "She has the same cut as her brother!"

"How bizarre!"

"What do you think this is?" I asked her shrilly. "This can't be right!"

She looked at me cluelessly.

"Menzire, what did they do to my children at that hospital?"

My father was equally alarmed when we showed him the wounds on the babies' necks. He immediately called the pediatric unit and demanded to speak with a doctor. "Unfortunately, all of our doctors are busy," the nurse on duty declared. "But if you can tell me your concern, perhaps I can help you."

"It's about my daughter Mihrigul Tursun's triplets."

"Just a moment. I need to get the medical files." There was a rustling sound on the other end of the line.

"Ah, I see. The children of Prisoner Tursusn. Okay…"

"I demand an explanation for the strange cuts on the children's necks."

The woman didn't reply.

"Did you hear me?"

"Yes."

"I'm calling about the cuts on their throats!"

"I'm sorry, but I don't see anything about that… All that is mentioned here is that the children didn't want to drink their formula and had to be fed artificially. They probably had to insert tubes into their stomachs."

"Through their necks?" My father was livid. "Do you think I believe that?"

"Please control yourself," the nurse urged placatingly. "Be glad that the children were even provided care here. They are foreigners, after all, so we weren't obligated to do so. You should be grateful to the Chinese government for that." She fired off an additional salvo of patriotic sayings but refused to divulge any additional information about the medical treatment the babies had received.

That night we all slept quite poorly. This was only partly because the babies kept waking up and wanted to be consoled. I was very restless myself. I anxiously watched over my two children and pondered what could have happened to them during my time in custody – especially to Mohammed, who was still stuck in the hospital.

At six o'clock, my father's phone went off. The screen indicated that the call was from the hospital, and he answered immediately.

"Yes? Yes," he said, and I noticed a shadow settle across his face. He shook his head, distraught. "How can that be?" he said. "Are you sure there hasn't been some mix-up?"

The voice on the other end said something, and then my father hung up. "What's wrong, Papa?" I asked. I was prepared for the bad news. "Has something happened to Mohammed?"

My father seemed incapable of speaking; he gazed at the floor and refused to raise his eyes. He finally cleared his throat. "They told me that Mohammed passed away during the night."

The news flashed through me like hot lightning. "No!" I contradicted him. That can't be true. My dear little Mohammed was dead? But we had just seen him yesterday!

My father placed his hand on my shoulder. "Come, we'll go to the hospital together," he said.

They were waiting for us in the pediatric ward. Besides the nurse with whom we had spoken the day before, two young doctors were waiting for us. One of them was Chinese, while the other was Uyghur. They gave us their condolences. "We did everything we could for your son, Ms. Tursun," the Chinese man declared. "But he simply wasn't strong enough."

The Uyghur doctor nodded in assent. "It isn't easy with triplets. And not all children are equally robust."

It all sounded implausible to my ears. Mohammed had been the strongest and sturdiest of the babies from the beginning. He had left my body first and was the largest of the three. And he, in particular, had supposedly not been strong enough to live?

"What was even wrong with him?" I managed to ask.

"His lungs were too weak, so we had to put him on a ventilator at the end."

"You saw this yourself yesterday," the nurse interjected.

We did try everything to save your child. You owe the Chinese government your gratitude."

The words of the doctors and nurse reached me as if through a veil. In some strange way, it all felt unreal, as if what was happening here had nothing to do with my child or me. Because there was no way my baby could be dead. I refused to accept this.

"Could you please release his body to us so we can properly bury my grandson?" I heard my father say. What was he talking about?

"Of course," the Uyghur doctor agreed. "We'll prepare the paperwork." I couldn't grasp what they were discussing, but I knew one thing with certainty though: my son wasn't dead.

A few minutes later, a woman from the hospital administration appeared and handed us a pile of documents, including Mohammed's death certificate and the hospital bill for his treatment, which I was supposed to sign. I refused. "There are nothing but lies on this!" I declared to my father as I defiantly pushed the papers away. He shot me a stern look.

"If you don't sign, I cannot hand your son over to you," the woman threatened.

"Just do it," my father urged me. I think he was scared that they would send me back to prison if I caused a scene at the hospital. In the end, he signed for me.

The woman was satisfied with that. "Good, now I'll go get him," she said, walking away.

When she returned, the woman was holding a bundle in her arms. Just like the children the hospital staff had brought me the day before, Mohammed was wrapped in a white blanket.

"There's my boy!" I exclaimed and moved to meet her.

The woman pressed the bundle into my arms. It was ice cold. I will never forget that chill surging throughout my body as I finally held my firstborn once more. I recognized him instantly; this baby with dark curls and a snub nose was my oldest son. He was as stiff as a board and cold, and his eyes were closed. But like the other two babies, he also had a strange cut across his throat.

I cradled him in my arms and gently caressed his tiny face. His cheeks tingled with cold. Undoubtedly, this baby had just been taken out of the freezer. And yet I still couldn't accept that he was dead. I asked the hospital employee to fetch me another blanket since I believed that if I could warm Mohammed up enough, he would wake up again. Wordlessly, she handed me the second blanket I had requested and then cordially asked us to leave the hospital.

"It'll be alright. The boy's just cold!" I told my father once we were seated in the taxi heading to the Ürümqi cemetery.

He didn't contradict me. "Yes, Mihrigul. Everything will be alright," he repeated.

CHAPTER 7

"Your God is Xi Jinping"

The Taklamakan Desert is located between Ürümqi and Qarqan, the Place of No Return, as we call it. My parents and I, along with the two babies, covered the 1,200 kilometers of nothingness composed of sand dunes and scorching summer heat on the bus all the way to our hometown of Qarqan. However, I have no recollection whatsoever of this journey.

The only thing I know is that I clutched the empty blanket the entire time, the one that had been wrapped around Mohammed until my father took my deceased son away to have him buried for me before our return to Qarqan. According to Islamic tradition, the burial should have occurred on the day of death. However, since we assumed that the baby had passed away some time ago, we wanted to have him buried as quickly as possible.

The only cemetery that was an option for us was the so-called Ürümqi Refugee Graveyard. This was where people who either weren't residents of Ürümqi or didn't have sufficient funds for a proper burial were interred. It was the only place we could procure a grave. What was even harder was finding an Imam to speak the prayers over the grave. My father canvassed various mosques, but all of the clerics were scared of the fallout that might ensue from doing the funeral, which was why he was turned down everywhere. Only after a long, desperate search did he track down two Imams willing to do the service for a "surcharge" equivalent to a little over two hundred dollars.

My aunt advised me to remain seated in the car as she and my father carried the baby into the cemetery, so I did that. When the people noticed that my parents wanted to bury a baby, many spoke up and offered to let them bury Mohammed among their relatives. In our faith, it is believed that babies who have died become angels, and if such an angel watched over a deceased person, there could be advantages. Most people hoped that this angel could alleviate possible suffering in hell. However, my father turned down all these offers because he didn't know the people personally and didn't want my son to end up in a grave with a criminal inadvertently.

And so they buried him in his own small plot. The two Imams read the appropriate Koranic surahs; nobody disrupted the ceremony. They then closed Mohammed's white eyes and scattered dirt and fresh flowers across my little angel. Today a gravestone bearing his name and his birth and death dates marks his resting place. Besides this, my father planted a chestnut tree there, which is flourishing despite the dry, dusty ground. I saw photos of this later on.

However, on the day itself, when my parents returned, I couldn't comprehend what was happening. I just clung despairingly to the blanket as if Mohammed was still wrapped in it. As we pulled onto the highway, I fussed: "Not so fast! The baby will wake up."

Since that day, I haven't been the same person. I left something precious behind in Ürümqi. Before that, I had been a person who loved life; I was self-confident and had plans. Now I am a mother who has lost her son.

I couldn't accept that my son had died for a long time. I still cannot, even to this day. Whenever someone asks me how many children I have, I always tell them three. And whenever their birthday comes around, I always buy three presents. I collect the gifts for my firstborn in a box and store them away. I tell the two younger children: "These are for your brother. We will give them to him when he comes back."

I know today that Mohammed will never return, but I didn't in those first few weeks after his death. I had completely lost my tether to reality. In our apartment in Qarqan, I sat for hours on end with the blanket in my arms, acting as if my baby was sleeping within its folds. I talked to him, fed him, and snapped at my aunt if she was too loud. "Be quiet!" I hissed. "Can't you see that Mohammed is sleeping?"

At first, she just watched me pityingly. She and my father were convinced I had lost my mind in the face of my little son's death. But at some point, it became too much for my aunt. All I did was sit around lethargically and talk to myself, and so one day, she revolted decisively against my fantasies. She snatched the blanket away from me and dramatically deposited it in the trash can in front of our building.

I raced out the door as if stung by a tarantula. "My baby!" I cried. "You threw away my baby!"

I tried to fish my precious blanket out of the garbage, but she blocked me and even gave me a light slap.

"Wake up!" she shouted at me. "That isn't a child. It's a blanket! It's time to accept that your son Mohammed is dead."

"Give me the blanket back right now!"

"No, it stays in the trash," she insisted. "And now go back inside and take care of your two other children. I can't do this alone anymore."

My aunt was stricter and more impatient with me than my father because as long as I was incapacitated, the main burden of caring for the children fell on her. "Your children need you," she told me. "They need a mother to care for them, not a mad woman." After this episode, I tried to pull myself together. Despite the fact that I often clashed with my aunt, I knew deep down that her accusations were justified. I think the main reason behind my reluctance to accept Mohammed's death was my sense of guilt. It felt as if I had failed as a mother. I was the one who had put him in danger; I hadn't been able to protect him. And to avoid facing these agonized thoughts, I took refuge in my fantasies.

Of course, I was also obliged to my two other children. By reminding me so emphatically of them, my aunt hit a nerve. It would be unforgivable if I also failed Elena and Moez by continuing to dwell in a space outside the bounds of reality solely due to the pain from my previous failure. The two children urgently needed my attention and love, and there was no way I could leave them in a lurch. "Do a better job this time, at least," I told myself. "Don't mess up again."

After adopting this attitude, I slowly succeeded at shaking off my paralysis and accepting my new reality, a bizarre reality. I now lived in a three-room apartment that my parents rented on the ground floor of a four-storied building. Until my arrival, my brother Ekper and his wife had lived here, having moved in after my younger sister Mihriban relocated to the distant province of Guangdong to attend college. However, the space became too crowded once I arrived with the children, so they moved in with my sister-in-law's parents, while my parents gave me and the children the second bedroom.

When I arrived with the children, there was no large family gathering or anything like that, as would have typically taken place. Especially whenever there was a new addition to the family, we usually threw large naming ceremonies. In my grandmother's village, I had been invited to many such parties as a child. I had, therefore, naturally assumed that my parents would also want to honor the birth of my children in the same way. But as I quickly realized, practically everything in my home region had changed during my absence. People now avoided gathering in larger groups out of concern that someone present there might have a problem with the authorities, which could create problems for the other attendees due to association. In my case, the situation was particularly dicey; my numerous aunts and uncles, cousins, nieces, and nephews all avoided me. They had heard that I had just been released from prison and was under police surveillance. As a result, people tended to give individuals like me a wide berth, so nobody came to see us.

And so, I led a very isolated life in Qarqan. Besides my parents, the only people I talked to were the police officers who took over my "case" after my arrival and supervised my house arrest. The officers frequently came by our apartment to question me. They kept wanting to know the same things over and over again: why I had been arrested in Ürümqi and what crime I had been accused of. They gave me a Huawei cell phone that I was instructed to keep turned on at all times. This way, they could keep tabs on my whereabouts and listen to my conversations. Everything I did with or in the presence of this device was recorded and then used as the basis for additional questions during my next interrogation. I couldn't call anyone on this phone except my parents. Besides being required to answer the constant check-in calls from the police, I was also strictly forbidden from doing anything on the internet.

Although I had been officially released from prison and formally declared "free," I could not communicate my situation to the outside world under these conditions. I could not contact other people in the city or friends outside of Xinjiang, including my foreign husband. Even if I could have disregarded the fact that my phone was meant only to serve the purposes of my watchers, I wouldn't have known how to contact Mahmud. I hadn't memorized his number, which had been saved to my Egyptian phone. And since we had only ever communicated via phone call and chat, I didn't have his email address either.

Since our parting at the Beijing airport, I could not speak with him or notify him about my situation. He knew nothing about my arrest or that I had been imprisoned for two months. Maybe he thought that, after my arrival in Ürümqi, I had traveled on to my parent's home as planned – and then dropped off the face of the planet. It could be that he even thought I had changed my mind in the face of my family's pressure and left him. How often had he tried to call the Egyptian phone the officers had confiscated? And what did he think of me? If he thought that I was staying in China of my own free will, along with the children, without notifying him, he probably considered me a traitor. That was my guess, at least. At the time, I had no idea that he was running into obstacle after obstacle at the Chinese embassy in Cairo in his attempts to obtain another entry visa.

I felt unbelievably guilty in terms of Mahmud. He was such a kind-hearted, responsible husband who had always been there for me when it mattered. And me? I was a complete failure as a wife. I had only caused him problems to date. What troubled me the most was the thought that I had something to confess to him, something just as unspeakable as it was unforgivable. I hadn't been able to tell him about our son's death.

I never spoke to my parents about these things. Since we were under ongoing surveillance, we only discussed innocuous topics such as the food or the weather – or we were just silent. My parents had also been given Huawei phones that they had to always keep with them. And so, like me, they lived in constant fear of being caught doing something that would seem suspicious to the police.

My father, who worked as a bus driver, was constantly being filmed as he moved along the streets since cameras were mounted everywhere throughout the city: at every street corner, intersection, and public square. This was why, for example, he stopped going to the mosque on Fridays, which he had otherwise regularly done. He hemmed, hawed, and pointed at his cell phone when I asked him about it. I understood; he was worried that he would get in trouble if the officers heard him saying prayers or if the cameras recorded him visiting the mosque.

These cameras were equipped with sensitive facial recognition software that could "read" emotions. They didn't just register who was going where and entering which buildings. They also registered whether the faces of the passersby looked worried or relaxed. The authorities interpreted worried faces as suspicious. As I later learned, the Uyghur people from Xinjiang were categorized according to a point system, in which only a full score ensured an existence untroubled by the police. Point deductions were taken for "offenses" such as visiting a mosque, saying prayers, reading from the Koran, wearing traditional clothing, traveling abroad, and having a large number of children. In the eyes of the authorities, all of these things were suspicious and required closer examination.

My father's clothing turned into his undoing. Since he was seriously balding by this point, he liked to wear an Uyghur cap decorated with colorful embroidery whenever he went outside. He had a small army of these at home and donned a different one every day, selecting them to match his outfits. However, these hats were outlawed soon after I moved in with my parents. Both the owning and the wearing of these caps were forbidden.

One day, there was a knock at our door, and we opened it to find two officers, one Chinese and one Uyghur, standing in front of it. At first, I thought that they were here for me as usual, but then they demanded to speak with my father. "He's at work," I explained truthfully.

"Is this your father?" the Uyghur officer asked as he showed me a photo of him behind a large steering wheel, wearing one of his colorful caps. I believe this image dates back to before the caps were forbidden, and my father had still been wearing them. Numerous cameras were bound to have caught him, so there was no point in denying anything.

"Yes, that's him," I replied.

The officers nodded. "Then we need to search your apartment." My heart plummeted because I knew what they were looking for and suspected they would find it. "Fine, take a look around," I heard myself say as I feverishly considered how I could keep them away from my father's closet. However, nothing came to me.

As if in a trance, I watched them search our apartment. They started in the hallway and systematically went from room to room. Already in the living room, they discovered several instruments that had been played at traditional festivals in our village. My father wasn't an avid musician, but he owned a rawap, a kind of lute, and a kushtar, a violin-like instrument played with a bow, belonging to his grandfather. As family heirlooms, these instruments were of huge, nostalgic value to my father.

The officers tore the rawap and the kushtar down from the hooks where he had mounted them to the wall. Then, they slammed the instruments onto the floor, the wood splintering everywhere. At that moment, my father arrived home and rushed into the living room. "What is going on here?" he shouted, staring in shocked disbelief at his destroyed instruments.

"What's going on here?" the Uyghur officer mimicked him. "We should be asking you the same thing!"

Only then did my father grasp the situation. "These are heirlooms...," he stammered.

It is forbidden to own instruments like this! You should have notified the precinct and handed them in," the officer declared. "We have on record that your household didn't participate in any of the neighborhood collection events."

According to the law, every household was obligated to relinquish traditional instruments and articles of clothing at a central collection site, where those items could be destroyed. However, my father had been unable to bring himself to do this. He had chosen to exile these pieces to the inside of our apartment – and had never reckoned on anyone searching our home. He now just stood there in mute dismay.

Meanwhile, the two officers continued their search with undiminished energy. They opened all the closets and cabinets, pulled out each and every drawer, and even looked under the beds to see if we had hidden anything there. And they struck gold! At the end of their raid, they dumped a considerable mountain of traditional shirts and caps next to the smashed instruments on our living room floor. And they even pulled an ancient Koran out of the topmost shelf in my father's closet.

"Just take a look at that," they mocked him. "Guess you didn't know that it's forbidden to keep a copy of the Koran in your home, did you?"

My father grew meeker and meeker. They confiscated all the instruments and clothes which meant so much to him. As for my father himself, they hauled him away to the police station for interrogation. And because my aunt and I were afraid that he might land in prison, too, we waited on pins and needles. If that happened, we would quickly find ourselves in dire straits because he was the only one of the five of us currently employed and earning money. I was banned from holding a job, and my aunt couldn't work because she had a kidney problem requiring dialysis treatment. How would we pay our future bills if my father didn't return home?

But he came back, fortunately. The following morning, he was escorted home by a Chinese officer in a black uniform. He didn't say a single word about how he had been treated, and we didn't ask. We knew this would worsen matters, so we were silent and acted as if nothing had happened.

The Chinese officer, however, flatly refused to leave. Instead, he installed himself in our living room – and remained there. In addition to our phones and the cameras on the streets, we now had someone watching over us day and night. This strange man filmed our family life without restraint, even when I was taking care of the children or helping my aunt in the kitchen. He kept bursting in everywhere to take video footage of us.

Through this behavior, he generated an atmosphere in which I felt as fragile as glass. It was almost like being back in prison, where cameras had been pointed at me all day long. Now it happened to me within my own four walls. Since I was under house arrest, I wasn't allowed to leave the apartment. Nonetheless, I could ask for permission to do things like go shopping at the market and take my children to the hospital. They needed medical treatment at this point. The man went with me whenever the central station gave me the green light to do these things.

He always walked a few steps behind, filming me the whole way. Neither of us ever talked, but on his phone, he provided live running commentary about what I was doing or planning to do to the central station. Even when I needed to consult with the doctors, he demanded to come with me and listen in.

"Of course, come in!" the pediatrician at the Qarqan hospital declared when my shadow wanted to trail me into the treatment room. "After all, we have no secrets from you!" Even the doctor knew the rules.

He examined my daughter's eyes – she now was severely cross-eyed – and recommended an operation. "If you treat this early enough, we can correct this malfunctioning," he said.

I nodded. "I would like to try that."

I asked him for a cost estimate since I was doubtful I could afford the treatment. Unlike Chinese citizens, my children didn't have health insurance that would cover the majority of their medical expenses. Just like foreigners, we Uyghurs had to pay for everything out of our pockets, which was why the hospital in Ürümqi handed me a hefty bill. I was supposed to pay 85,000 yuan, equivalent to 10,000 dollars, for my children's "treatment" there. I considered this a travesty; they hadn't only killed my first-born child but were demanding payment from me. I now carried a certificate of debt around with me and had no idea how I would pay it. This was why each new treatment for the children entailed increased financial hardship.

The doctor eventually turned his attention to my son, whose head was still much too large. He couldn't provide a definitive explanation for what had caused this. I also reported to him that the baby was frequently short of breath and prone to coughing. "His lungs are probably undersized, and he needs more oxygen," the doctor said as he listened to Moez's chest with a stethoscope. He eventually diagnosed my son as having bronchopulmonary dysplasia and recommended that I bring him to the hospital every four days for oxygen treatments. This would be especially critical for further developing my baby's brain.

I stared at him in astonishment. Was he trying to tell me my child would be mentally debilitated if I didn't bring him for this treatment? "What would this cost?" I asked in a panic.

He named a price, and I gulped. I was now certain that we would have to sell my father's car and Menzire's gold jewelry to cover all our medical procedures.

"And how did he get this disease, Doctor?" I asked him as we walked out.

He hemmed and hawed. "It isn't all that uncommon in prema-ture babies," he finally said.

"But the children were completely healthy when they were born!"

"Yes, but they were artificially fed and ventilated during their separation from you." He looked nervous at my shadow, pointing his camera at us again. "And when that happened, his lungs could have... gotten inflamed."

"From the equipment?"

"That would be hard to diagnose in retrospect," he choked out, twisting his head out of the video being taken by the officer. "In any case, I highly recommend this treatment for your son."

With those words, he bade me goodbye. Walking home with both children in my arms, I racked my brain over how my father and I could scrounge together enough to pay the astronomical sum to cover my debts in Ürümqi: my aunt's treatment, Elena's recommended eye operation and the oxygen treatments for my son. We would probably have to beg our relatives and attempt to convince them to sell some of their lands so that they could lend us money.

Our family's financial situation was already precarious, even without this additional burden. Since the powdered milk for the children was so expensive, I often opted to buy flour and dissolve it in water to satisfy them. Of course, I knew this wasn't a particularly healthy form of nourishment, but I couldn't even afford diapers, considering the thinness of my father's wallet. So instead, I wrapped the babies in pieces of cotton fabric that could be laundered. This was arduous since I had to wash out the diapers constantly, but this was just how it was.

Once again, I yearned to contact Mahmud in some way so that he could help support me. I was firmly convinced that he would do that for his children regardless of what he thought of me. But it was as if the police had cast an invisible spell around me, effectively cutting me off from the rest of the world. I found myself still imprisoned while I lived with my parents; it was just against a different backdrop and under somewhat more bearable circumstances than had existed in my prison cell. The only comfort I had during this gray period came from the sight and smiles of my two babies, Moez and Elena, who were slowly growing larger and stronger despite all the odds.

Everything changed drastically one day in April 2017. Although I scrupulously adhered to all the rules and tried to stay free from all blame, four police officers with dogs stormed into our apartment one day. They kicked open the door with a loud crash while we were all still in bed. My two children, who were almost two by that point, were tucked in next to me. They were terrified when the men suddenly surrounded our bed, and their dogs barked at us. They started to scream in fear.

The officers explained that I was being placed under arrest. Then, under the frightened gazes of my children and my father, who had rushed into my bedroom, they handcuffed me. "Come with us" was the order.

I was completely dumbfounded. "But... what for?" I stammered.

"No questions," one of the officers snarled. "We will discuss this some more at the station."

I expected them to tape up my mouth again and cover my head with a sack, but they didn't do that this time. Our neighbors had overheard everything that had happened – and were probably meant to. Everyone knew where I was being taken.

They transported me by van to the main police headquarters in Qarqan, a large gray administrative building. Many other hand-cuffed Uyghurs were already gathered in the police yard, and the officers led them inside the building. This was a second wave of cleansing. All "suspicious persons" who were already under sur-veillance by the police were being re-arrested. We were told that each "case" was being reopened.

The officers grabbed me roughly by the handcuffs and dragged me into a subterranean interrogation room, which, like the one in Ürümqi, had no windows. Harsh, white lights were burning in this room, and all sorts of terror-inducing instruments were hung up along the walls. These were tools of torture. I knew instantly that they would be used to inflict pain on the other prisoners and me. I recognized this even if I didn't exactly understand how each one of them functioned – and I was terribly scared of what lay ahead of me.

The officers strapped me to a so-called tiger bench. You had to sit on this very narrow bench with outstretched legs. My legs were extended straight in front of me, parallel to the floor, while my hands were cuffed behind a backrest so that my torso was tightly stretched. It was an extremely uncomfortable, unnatural position. At first, it was alright, but it didn't take long for you to start feeling severe pain in your limbs and overextended joints.

While in this position, the officers started to interrogate me. This time it was two Uyghurs and one Chinese man in a green uniform who stood in a semicircle around me. The Chinese officer led the interrogation, armed with a pile of documents; all the notes and records the police had gathered over the past few years were at his fingertips. He knew everything about me, but that didn't keep him from repeatedly asking me the same basic questions: "Where were you born? How old are you? Where did you go to school? Are you Muslim? Why did you choose to study abroad?"

Early on, I could still concentrate reasonably well, but at some point, the incessant repetition and my horribly uncomfortable condition wore me down. I began to fidget on the bench as I grew weary. That earned me a slap, and the officers tightened the straps so that I no longer had any room for movement. In addition, they shoved a board under my feet to increase the tension in my muscles. It was excruciating.

Meanwhile, they continued the interrogation without skipping a beat. The bright lamp seared my eyes, and I replied to their questions like a robot. I gave them the same answers over and over again, but the longer the interrogation lasted, the more tired and confused I became. I also lost all feeling in my body as my hands and feet went numb. And then I must have dozed off because I was shocked when someone hit me hard on the back of the head.

"You aren't allowed to sleep!" the officers shouted at me. However, they were no longer the ones who had initially interrogated me. These were different individuals, although they wore the same uniforms and asked me the same questions. And they also had dogs with them that barked threateningly, which rattled me. My answers became increasingly confused. I began to get muddled up, despite the fact that everything we were covering were topics that I had already talked about a thousand times. Whenever I messed up my response, they spat on and slapped me. My right ear went numb as a result of that. "See, you're contradicting yourself! You're trying to deceive us," they claimed. "Why don't you just tell us the truth?"

When I fell asleep a second time, they threw a bucket of water in my face. I greedily licked at the droplets because I was incredibly thirsty and hadn't drunk anything for many hours. They hit me in the face repeatedly until I felt very dizzy and could no longer hear anything out of my right ear. At that point, I realized other prisoners were in the room with me. They were also being tortured. I then passed out again. My body desperately needed a break, but they wouldn't give me even one second of peace. They kept beating me whenever my eyes closed. "Allah, let me die!" I begged silently, though I never uttered it aloud.

The men finally ordered me to open my mouth, and the Chinese officer forced a pill into my mouth. I panicked. What was this? Did he intend to kill me? I desperately tried to spit it out, but the Chinese man yanked my chin up with practiced ease, and another officer poured a glass of water into my mouth. This triggered my swallowing reflex, and the pill slid right down my throat.

I instantly felt its effect. Some drug instantly relaxed me; I suddenly stopped feeling scared. The fact that the officers around me were flicking their cigarette butts into my face no longer felt menacing. Their dogs continued to bark, but so what? What did that matter to me? They watched my reaction, shone a flashlight into my eyes, and resumed their questioning.

"Do you have any contacts abroad? Are you Muslim? Are you a terrorist? Do you pray?" they asked. And then, more specifically: "Since your incarceration in Ürümqi, have you prayed in your parents' home? Admit it!"

"Yes, I'm Muslim, and I do pray," I replied since, under the influence of the pill, I no longer felt any reason to conceal my religious beliefs from them. Besides, they knew everything about me as it was. And yes, I had prayed at home and implored God to help my ailing children. There was no point in denying any of this. As I confessed these things, I felt oddly superior to them. At least as long as the pill was still effective. "My God is stronger than yours," I declared recklessly.

This infuriated them. "Really?" the Chinese officer cried angrily. "We'll see about that! Call on your god to save you. If he's as strong as all that."

The other men laughed.

"Allah! Let me die!" I now shouted the prayer I had been silently uttering the entire time. I could no longer bear the agony in the basement of torture, which had stretched on for days already. "Please, please kill me!"

I waited for Allah to intervene and perhaps render me unconscious. But nothing like that happened. Instead, the Chinese man just grew angrier and angrier. "Your religion is the Communist Party, and your god is Xi Jinping!" he screamed. "Haven't you learned that yet? After all the education you've received?" He was probably referring to my previous incarceration. "Repeat after me: my religion is the Communist Party, and my god is Xi Jinping."

I recognized this slogan from the brainwashing program at the Ürümqi prison. And I loathed him. I despised all the Chinese. I vehemently shook my head. "God will punish you! He will punish all of you!" I bellowed at the men.

The Chinese officer grimaced angrily once more. Then he gave an order to his Uyghur comrades, and they strapped on my head a kind of helmet from the side of which dangled cables they could use to transmit electricity via remote control. They attached electrodes to my hands and feet as well. I could guess what was about to follow.

"Now, let's see who is going to punish whom here! We will be the ones punishing you, not the other way around," the Chinese officer announced grimly.

He didn't promise more than he delivered. A jolt was already flashing through my body, from my head downward. Excruciating pain shot through me from top to bottom, momentarily robbing me of my ability to breathe. The men watched as my body twitched, then they sent another shock through me that was a little stronger than the first. As it went through me like a whiplash, I whimpered in anguish. "Kill me! Allah, kill me," I sobbed. But this only antagonized them all the more, and they kept sending more shocks through me.

"My religion is the Communist Party, and my god is Xi Jinping. Say it!" the Chinese officer insisted obsessively.

But after all I'd been through, I hardly had the strength to reply. I laboriously stammered something. "That wasn't clear enough!" he criticized me, sending another shock through me. It was never enough. The three officers tortured me with electric shocks until I lost consciousness.

When I woke up, a man in a doctor's coat was kneeling beside me and taking my pulse. I found myself in a brightly lit infirmary. "She's awake," he said to the officer who was standing beside him.

I was stretched out on a cot with shackles around my wrists. Close by, I saw another woman with the same welts on her body as I had, so I assumed that she must have also been bound to a tiger bench. Several uniformed officers, men and women were in the room with us.

A nurse removed my clothing so that the doctor could examine me. He studied the welts on my body, palpated my organs, took a blood sample, looked down my throat, and demanded that I breathe deeply for his stethoscope. I was completely exhausted and submissive, so I let him do all this.

However, the doctor then told me to spread my legs. I hesitated, but two officers were already stepping toward me and forcibly prying my legs apart. They bound my legs to the legs of the cot so that the doctor could access my pubic area easily from underneath. And that is exactly what he did. He was holding some kind of pliers in his hand, and I instantly felt panic-stricken. My weakness evaporated in a flash, and I tried to lash out but couldn't move because the officers had shackled my hands and feet. They were also holding me by the abdomen now as well.

The doctor opened my vagina with some metal instrument and pitilessly spread apart my labia. I screamed as a piercing pain shot through me. I don't know what the doctor did inside me, but it felt like he had ripped or sliced something out of me – without any anesthesia. The pain was horrific.

The officers released my shackles after that. "Stand up," they ordered.

But I was in no condition to do that. The pain was too intense, and my legs buckled as soon as I tried to get on my feet. I also noticed blood running down my legs, although neither the doctor nor the nurse who had treated me seemed to care.

The officers supported me from both sides because I couldn't keep myself upright. They handed back to me my pants and t-shirt and helped me to get dressed again. As soon as this was accomplished, they pulled another black sack over my head, then loaded three other prisoners and me into a parked and ready van in the police yard.

They didn't drive us far. I couldn't see where they were taking us at the time, but today I know that the new camp was only four kilometers from my parent's apartment. They apparently knew where I was being kept, too, or at least learned about it later. They told me subsequently that they had occasionally dropped off food there.

This new camp was a gigantic complex, which the residents of Qarqan gave a wide berth to keep from landing there themselves. You could see practically nothing from the outside since the area was shielded by a tall wall topped by barbed wire—a huge, multi-story building shaped like an L was concealed behind it. The main entrance, as well as the offices for the prison administration and the centralized guard unit, were located at the corner formed by the two arms of the L. The prison cells ran along both sides of the two lengths. There was no yard area.

They took us, the three newcomers, into a room with a large mirrored wall where other prisoners who had also recently arrived were already waiting. There they removed the sacks from our heads. We were told to take off our clothes again, the men and the women. Once we had all stripped naked, we were instructed to line up in front of the mirror and spread our arms and legs.

I studied myself in the midst of the other damaged bodies, all of whom had Uyghur features like mine. But I no longer recognized myself in the crowd. Was that really me? The woman with the swollen face, who was still dripping blood from her abdomen? Was I even still a person? How had I gotten into this situation? And what had the doctor just done to me?

As I stared stubbornly ahead, the officers took my measurements. They measured the length of my arms, legs, chest circumference, and height. The other prisoners underwent the same procedure. Then they ordered us to bend forward. I felt someone roughly grab my braid from behind and slice it off with a loud snip. It fell away from me onto the floor. I then felt the buzzing of an electric razor touch my neck and watched as the fluff of my dark hair sailed down all around my head.

"Stand up straight," shouted the voice of an officer.

And so I straightened up and gazed once more into the mirror. I found myself staring at someone who was a complete stranger. That wasn't Mihrigul Tursun anymore. She was some anonymous female prisoner with shorn hair.

After this procedure, they passed out our uniforms, which were sewn from the same blue fabric as the one I had worn during my first incarceration. The coarse fabric smelled like chemical cleaners and chafed my skin. I had very clear memories of this fabric and couldn't believe I had to wear it again. My uniform was marked with the number 17. Once I was dressed, they shackled my hands and feet. I was already acquainted with the handcuffs, but the foot shackles were a new, very uncomfortable experience. They severely limited my range of motion, so I could only take little shuffling steps. The guards once again yanked a sack over my head.

They accompanied me into the basement. With each step I took, the shackles bit into my ankles. What was I doing in the basement? Were they going to lock me into another lightless cell down here? The memory of my time in isolation triggered a wild panic inside me. I knew I would lose my mind if I had to go through that again. This was why I was relieved when, after a short distance, we took a staircase heading upward.

The guards led me out of the central section, down a long corridor flanked on both sides by prison cells. They eventually came to a stop and removed my sack. We were standing in front of cell number 210. They unlocked the door and shoved me inside.

I will never forget the unimaginably foul stench inside that cell. It was packed full of women who hadn't been allowed to wash for months.

"You smell so nice!" exclaimed one of the women, who had very pale skin, freckles, and short, crazy hair. She pressed her nose against my arm and sniffed it like a flower. This was despite the fact I had just been released from three days of interrogation and torture. Nonetheless, compared to the others here, I probably smelled good. "When we get out of here, we will all smell just a sweet," the woman declared. "And that won't be much longer!" I saw how some of the other inmates rolled their eyes at this.

"Aygul is a little crazy, but she's a good soul," a girl whispered. She had high cheekbones, a snub nose, and large, round teenage eyes; as I later discovered, her name was Dilnaz. I wondered how such a young girl had landed here.

"Quiet in there!" the two women were warned via the loud-speaker. All the women fell silent.

In many aspects, the new prison in Qarqan was organized along the same lines as the one I had been in Ürümqi. Here, too, we were watched around the clock by cameras and guards who told us what we were supposed to do. They also monitored our success at memorizing the Red Book and disciplined us whenever we said something wrong. The cameras were mounted in all four corners of the room so that regardless of where you were located, they always had eyes on you.

However, the prison conditions in this second camp were considerably harsher than in the first. It began with forty women crammed into our forty-square-meter cell. We had incredibly little space in there. Standing anywhere without brushing against the other women around you was impossible. It was as if we were driving around in a stinky, overcrowded bus that never made any stops but instead just kept taking on new passengers. Because it didn't just end with the forty inmates; a steady stream of new inmates were brought to our cell. The number of women in my cell eventually reached 62. I know this sounds unimaginable to those who haven't experienced it, but that is how it was. And I would genuinely never wish for anyone to have to experience what this was actually like.

There was always a certain degree of attrition, though. Some women couldn't withstand the hardship. Periodically someone would collapse and have to be carried out of the cell by the officers. A few of them returned, but not all. Twelve of my cellmates died during the two months I was there. It wasn't astonishing in light of the fact we didn't only suffer from malnutrition but from permanent sleep deprivation.

Our cell was so crowded that we had to take turns sleeping in shifts. The women on the first shift could stretch out on the floor and rest between 10 p.m. and 1:30 a.m. Then, in the middle of the night, the groups changed places, and those who stood for the first shift received the coveted spaces on the floor to rest a little.

Our daily routine was strictly regimented. We were woken up at five o'clock in the morning by the loudspeakers and had to greet each new day with a song. "Socialism is good. Socialism is the light that shines across our people. Socialism has provided us with good food, nice clothes, and a good life," we sang. "A great China is good. We strive to be the greatest China in the world."

The first item in our daily routine was using the latrine, which took an hour and a half since there were so many of us. As in the other camp, we had to defecate into a hole in the floor. Right after getting up, we formed a line to use it, one after the other, under everyone's gaze (including that of the cameras). Some women were always in a hurry to reach the hole after a long night. I was one of them due to the bladder control problems I had suffered from since the birth of my children. This had been an issue during my first incarceration as well. However, now the problem was compounded because I wasn't granted any additional trips to the hole beyond the three that were on the daily schedule.

"Just shit in your pants!" was the loudspeaker's advice when I asked to use the hole the night after my arrival.

This was why I felt I would explode if I didn't get to the hole immediately. One of my fellow prisoners, a stout woman with dark skin and dark, shoulder-length hair, noticed my predicament the first morning after my arrival. She stood at the front of the line and let me go ahead of her. The others grumbled quietly about how they were never given special treatment. The woman with dark skin ignored them; I shot her a grateful glance, and she gave a little smile.

Once at the hole, however, I realized how difficult it was to pull my pants down while handcuffed. I was only able to achieve this after all sorts of laborious contortions. The other women were beginning to push and shove as I did this, in part because not everyone in our cell wore these shackles. This additional annoyance was reserved for only about a dozen women; the others had little sympathy for our plight.

I squatted down but could not place my shackled feet on either side of the hole. I could only crouch down in front of the hole and push my rear as far out as possible without tipping over. I just barely hit the hole without soiling myself. I was hardly done before my cellmates started shoving again.

"Hey, you can't spend all day taking a shit," the next woman in line hissed at me. I understood they were all nervous because they were scared they wouldn't have a turn if we took too long. And yet, I was still standing there with my pants around my ankles. Despite my cuffs, I tried desperately to pull them up. I was terribly embarrassed when I couldn't seem to manage that. I then felt someone brush against the back of my leg and then yank my pants up with a hearty tug. It was, once again, the woman with dark skin who had let me in front of her.

"Thank you," I mumbled, feeling ashamed. She nodded.

"What's your name?" I asked.

"Nur."

"Mine's Mihrigul."

"Silence, numbers 17 and 23!" the voice from the loudspeaker interjected, and we immediately stopped talking.

After the latrine event, we received the next set of instructions. "Make your bed!" That was something of a joke. Each woman instantly reached for the sheet she had used the night before. It had to be folded down to the size of an A5 piece of paper, and the final product had to be completely smooth without wrinkles and with perfect corners.

This task was practically impossible to do with my hands cuffed. I tried to produce what was asked for, but even when I used my teeth, I could not hand in the ideal shape. My rectangle was a little lopsided and had a tiny wrinkle at its edge. I couldn't get it any better than that on the fly. Nonetheless, I handed it over at the cell entrance as required.

Then a delegation of ten high-ranking camp officials appeared at our cell door. We greeted the delegation in a militaristic fashion. We sang a song to the best of our abilities, praising the struggle of the Chinese working class and the glorious victory of the Communist Party. I already knew this song from my previous prison stay. "Without the Communist Party, there would be no New China. Without the Communist Party, China would never have completed this difficult task," we sang as we balled our right hands into fists to emphasize the lyrics by stretching them combatively into the air. "The National Communist Party has created a new China. It smoothed the path to liberation for the people, and it has led China to a better future. The new China was built to provide its people with the best life possible."

After that, the delegation inspected our folded sheets piled on the floor next to the cell door. I felt a little queasy when I realized how closely they examined them. "This one's sloppy!" I heard one of the officials declare. "Who did this?"

Oh no! He was holding up my sheet as he wrinkled his nose at it disapprovingly.

"Number 17," the loudspeaker blared.

"Number 17, step forward!" the official bellowed.

My knees quaking, I stepped forward. The uniformed official glanced back and forth between me and my sheet, then pulled it back and hit me across the face with it like a club. I stood there stoically. "What made you think you could hand in such sloppy work?" he thundered.

I gazed mutely at the floor. "As punishment, you will fold your sheet one hundred times," the warden declared.

My cellmates once again lined up as two guards carried in a tub of rice water for our breakfast. Every woman had to recite a saying before receiving a cup of it. The first woman rattled off, "*Harkuni agtiganda tamakyiyishten burdun damimiz....*" The full quote went as follows: "To give with generosity, to stand against death, to admit to crimes, and to not break the law – this will prevent the worst and most shameful of deaths."

Before long, I knew the passage by heart just from hearing it, but when I reached the front of the line, the guards refused to give me a cup. "You don't deserve any breakfast! You have to learn how to fold your sheet first," they exclaimed.

This game repeated itself at lunch. When all the others received a small piece of steamed bread, the guards denied me my ration because I had allegedly not made enough progress in my folding during the morning. It was straight-up harassment. Nur was once again standing behind me, and I could feel her sympathetic gaze on my neck. "I'm sure you'll learn it quickly," she murmured in my direction. These were only a few hastily whispered words, but I was immensely glad that at least one person was willing to speak to me in this hell hole and try to console me.

Nur became my friend. We communicated primarily with our eyes because this contact was the only one our watchers behind the cameras didn't explicitly sanction. Through our eyes, we silently commented on what was happening while also forging an invisible connection with others. It was a secret, complicit form of friendship that could have only existed in this very specific situation.

We frequently tried to get close to each other. In the mornings, she helped me with lowering and raising my pants. And when we lined up at the cell door to accept our meager rations of bread or rice from our guards, she often slipped into line right in front of or behind me. During our march-in-place exercises and other militaristic activities, we were assigned positions that weren't far apart. At night, Nur always held a spot for me so I could fall asleep with my back against one side of her body or the other. I don't know if the other women or our guards picked up on our complicity, but we both took care of each other in an attempt to secretly preserve one last remnant of interpersonal relationships.

The Red Book also played a critical role in this camp, and most of our time was consumed with studying it. The books sat, neatly stacked one on top of the other, against our cell wall. When we reached a particular point in the afternoon, the loudspeaker would order us to line up again, this time in twos or threes, to get one of the copies. Nur needed my help with reading and memorizing the texts. As a country girl, she had only attended school for a few years, so she could hardly decipher any Chinese characters.

"What is the source of all evil?" I read to her softly. "Separatism, terrorism, extremism."

She repeated the words after me in a murmur. "Separatism, terrorism and, uh…" She looked at me questioningly.

"… extremism."

She nodded sadly. "The police think I'm an extremist," she said softly.

"I know," I replied. "They think we all are."

We were never allowed to exchange more than a few words with each other. Nonetheless, I gradually learned Nur's story. She was a country woman who had married young and never traveled outside our province. By the time she reached her mid-twenties, she'd had three young children: two, four, and six years old. She had already spent over a year in prison, which explained her shoulder-length hair. I was puzzled by her longer incarceration because I couldn't see why she would be of much "interest" to the authorities. After all, unlike me, they could hardly accuse her of being in contact with foreign Islamists.

However, Nur had a different problem; her entire family was imprisoned. Her brother had decided at some point to turn his back on his homeland and go to Afghanistan, and after that happened, all of his immediate relatives were arrested. Nur's younger brother had been slapped with a ten-year prison sentence, while her husband had been sentenced to sixteen years. Nur's father and mother were also behind bars. Despite all this, Nur hadn't calculated on being arrested herself. After all, she led a very inconspicuous life in her village.

When two police officers had appeared at her home demanding that she come with them to the police station, she had been in the process of feeding sugar beets to her three sheep. The men had sworn that her interrogation wouldn't last long, so Nur had left her children playing in the garden and had followed them in her farmwife's clothing. That was the last time she saw either her children or her farm. "I still have no idea what has happened to them," she confessed to me one night as we leaned against each other on the floor, and her mouth was very close to my ear. At night, we could sometimes communicate a bit more. "Can you even imagine how bad I feel about them?"

"There was nothing you could do."

"Yes, but I was responsible for them." She began to weep softly – and I was worried that the two of us might get in trouble. I wanted to comfort her, but what could I say to her?

"If I get out of here before you do, I'll go look for them."

"Do you promise?"

"By Allah," I vowed, and she sighed in relief. But I had no idea how I could possibly fulfill this promise. And I failed to uphold my promise, however hard it is for me to confess this. So to this day, I carry this guilt with me.

When it came time to memorize the texts from the Red Book, other "students" often joined Nur and me. Aygul, the woman with the green eyes and the face full of freckles who had commented on how good I smelled the day I arrived, and Dilnaz, the teenager who had been described as "crazy" because of her babbling commentary. The two of them regularly sat down with us, listened as I read the texts aloud, and quietly explained their meaning. We often functioned as a study group of four in which I was both teacher and translator for the others.

Sometimes we had to memorize texts that personally spoke to us. "How do you feel in prison, where your life is hard?" I recall this as the title of one of the poems we read. "First, you were a good boy or girl, and your parents worked hard for you. The state financed your future. Your parents thought you were a strong person, as strong as a horse. Your country wanted you to love it, but have you considered it? Consider how you have responded to your fatherland!" The second part of this poem was particularly painful since it appealed to our conscience and our responsibility to our families. "Your parents would like you to return home and open the door," it declared. "They want you to return to them as quickly as possible and embrace them. I hope that they are doing as well as you think they are! Dear friend, what has become of you? Do your parents deserve such a child who has broken the law? Do they deserve children who have no future?"

Whenever I repeated those sentences, my parents frequently came to mind. I could not stop that from happening or keep myself from brooding: What had I done to them? Had it been necessary for me to go abroad to study? The Communist Party had indeed given me an excellent education in China! Why couldn't I have just been content with that? In moments like that, I truly believed in its content while I marched in place and repeated that text for the umpteenth time. Yes, the Communist Party had wanted only the best for my future, I thought. But I had rejected its offer, proving myself to be ungrateful. That was why I only had myself to blame for my fate. I began to feel like that back then as the daily brainwashing started to take effect.

Aygul had a particularly hard time repeating the texts, especially when she had to say them on her own. She didn't know a word of Chinese, so whenever she tried to utter the words, she usually got all tangled up. And sometimes, her sentences sounded so absurd that we all had to laugh, even despite our terrible situation. This was Aygul's superpower; she could boost our spirits and inspire something that resembled confidence in our cell. Unlike many other women who despaired in their situation, she always walked around with her head high. She refused to let anyone intimidate her, even though she often got in trouble for this.

Aygul was phenomenal; she was always full of energy, and even in the most difficult of moments, she could trot out cool quotes and sayings. She refused ever to show fear or pain to our guards. Once, when she couldn't correctly recite a lesson from the Red Book, the guards beat her in front of all of us. But afterward, instead of letting herself be intimidated, she said, "These assholes will get what's coming to them. Believe me, girls! Our men will come and take us out of here soon. And then they'll be the ones whimpering for mercy!" She couldn't have cared less that our guards were listening to every word she said through the cameras. Some women were convinced she was crazy because of this, but I think this was Aygul's personal strategy for coping with our situation. She could have just sat in a corner and cried, but instead, she chose not to dwell on her despair. Not even once did she admit to any form of weakness or fragility.

Aygul had caught the attention of the authorities because her father and her brother lived abroad. I think this fed her expectation that some help would eventually come from that direction. I have no idea what happened to her husband; Aygul never said much about him. She was also reticent when it came to her two children. I assumed that the thought of them was too painful, even for a fighter like her. For us mothers, there was nothing more agonizing than separation from our children.

Dilnaz was the only one in our circle who wasn't married and hadn't left behind children at the time of her arrest. She had been a tenth-grade student at the high school in Qarqan before her chat contacts with individuals outside of China had gotten her in trouble. Dilnaz had actively sought out these contacts because she dreamed of traveling. She asked me over and over again what it was like to fly in a plane, and she couldn't imagine how nor-mal-sized humans could fit in such a small contraption. "A plane like that is bigger than our cell," I told her. "Why shouldn't just as many people fit inside of it?" Her eyes grew huge at this. At just seventeen years of age, she was still very naive and looked quite young. Unfortunately, this made her desirable in the eyes of our guards.

One evening, Dilnaz was raped by the uniformed men. She was sobbing horribly when they shoved her back into the cell the next morning, and she was bleeding from her vagina. I think she had been a virgin at the time of her arrest. She never said a word about what the men had done to her, but her injuries made it abundantly clear. The countless scratches running down her arms revealed she had tried to fight them off with every ounce of strength. It made me unbelievably sad. I wanted to console her, but I couldn't think of anything to say to her. It was all so dreadful that I couldn't find any uplifting words.

As usual, Aygul didn't find herself at a loss for words. "Just wait! Those assholes will get what's coming to them!" she promised Dilnaz, who flashed a weak smile before a dark shadow settled across her face again. This shadow never left her side after that. It was as if her naiveté evaporated, and she never again asked me what it was like to travel on a plane.

This didn't remain an isolated incident. One week later, they fetched Dilnaz again. She was returned the following morning, sobbing once more and severely battered. Her injuries were even worse than they had been the first time. "Those who beat you like that are pigs!" Aygul loudly declared to the cameras. However, she was soon made to pay for this commentary.

On one of the next evenings, the guards took away Dilnaz and Aygul, whose fair complexion also made her attractive to them. "We're going to teach you a lesson – and then you'll learn to hold your tongue," they said.

That night neither Nur nor I slept a wink; we were terribly afraid for our friends. We lay on the floor with our bodies pressed together, breathlessly listening to see if we could hear any sounds of them from the other side of the wall. I was mostly worried for Dilnaz because she was still so young and had been so severely mistreated the first two nights that the guards had assaulted her.

"Hopefully, they will get tired of them soon," Nur whispered.

"Hopefully," I agreed with her sadly. However, I knew in all likelihood that this wouldn't be the case. It was more like the guards had their preferences. They kept taking the same girls repeatedly to use throughout the night. It was usually the youngest and prettiest of the women they picked out, but generally speaking, no women in the camp were safe from sexual violence.

Nur and I were fortunate that we had been spared thus far. As I only found out later, in my case, that was because my prison file bore a notation that I had a venereal disease. I had my uncle, who worked for the Qarqan police force, to thank for that. But at the time, I didn't know and felt just as vulnerable as all the other women.

Nur assumed that the men weren't interested in her because she had been suffering from constant bleeding for months. Our guards knew about this because the blood seeped through her pants, which by this point were all dark and stiff with dried blood. The guards found this state of affairs not quite so attractive, and therefore she, just like me, was left alone, at least in a sexual sense. Thank God.

I suspect that Nur's bleeding was a side effect of the drugs they were giving us. Once a week, our guards handed us a white pill and our evening rice ration. First, one of the men would force our mouths open and stick them inside. Next, a second man would pour a cup of water after it, and then the first man would shove his finger into our mouths to verify that we weren't hiding the pill underneath our tongues or between our teeth. This was very unpleasant, but they apparently wanted to ensure we swallowed the pills.

No one told us what purpose these pills served or what effects they caused. However, according to the rumors, these drugs were to meant to render us infertile. The women in our cell talked about this among themselves. We all sensed that the pills were affecting our menstrual cycles. However, for most of the women, myself included, the drug's effect was the opposite of what happened to Nur. From the moment we started taking the pills, our periods abruptly ended.

We waited the following morning for our friends to return. After the two previous rapes, they brought Dilnaz back to us during the morning latrine lineup. This was why Nur and I grew nervous when they still hadn't appeared by the time of the morning sheet inspection. "What's taking them so long?" my friend murmured to me.

I shot her a perplexed glance, and then we had to continue our task. We were ordered to jog around the perimeter of the cell. This was unbelievably painful for all the other women wearing shackles around our feet, including me, because the metal cut into our skin, which was already rubbed raw. I gritted my teeth as I shuffled along. Since everyone who wasn't shackled could run faster than I and the cell was overcrowded as it was, it was easy to trip. I often wound up on the floor and had to get back on my feet quickly to prevent others from trampling me.

When the smashup was finally over, the cell door swung open, and Aygul was pushed back into us. She landed on all fours and instantly started to swear. "Those fucking bastards...." I heard her growl – and I could hardly hold back a smile. I thought this woman went through something terrible last night, but they didn't break her. But where was our other friend? "What's going on with Dilnaz?" I asked her quietly.

"Dilnaz is dead. Those bastards killed her," Aygul replied quite loudly.

I stared at her in bewilderment. Her green eyes were turbulent, like a storm-tossed sea. But, at that very moment, I knew she was telling the truth. Our friend hadn't survived the night.

"Shut the fuck up, you bitch!" someone shouted through the loudspeaker. "If you don't, you know what's in store for you!" It was a blatant threat, but Aygul refused to be cowed by it.

"Those assholes murdered her," she continued. "Dilnaz is now out of all this…."

None of the other women in the cell said a word. They just stared at Aygul and bit their hands. We always did this if we didn't want to scream out loud or break down in tears. We pushed our fists into our mouths and stifled every sound within us.

Nur's bleeding grew increasingly worse. I don't know what was wrong with her. She was bleeding so heavily toward the end that all the color in her face drained away. She looked like a ghost and urgently needed medical care. Whenever the guards brought our meals, she asked them over and over again to see a doctor, but her pleading fell on deaf ears. The guards ignored her condition.

But then, one day, after we had spent almost two months together in that hell, they suddenly ordered her to come with them. They handcuffed my friend, pulled a sack over her head, and led her away. I felt awful watching this happen because Nur was like my sister, and I had no idea what they planned to do to her. Was she finally going to get the medical treatment she longed for? Or did they want to interrogate her? What did they intend to do to her? After all, I had been through here; I knew that anything was possible at any given time, from sexual assault to psychological and physical torture. They could do whatever they wanted to us, which is what they did.

I fearfully awaited Nur's return. Normally, the women who were being interrogated were gone for an entire day. Or a night if the guards had other plans for them. However, Nur didn't return. She had now been gone for two days. I hoped they might have released or taken her to another camp. It was possible; after all, she wasn't a dangerous person. Maybe the officers had finally grasped this fact after terrorizing and watching her for over a year.

More than anything, I wished my friend could return to her village and see her children again. She had been so worried about the three of them. As she had told me repeatedly, "Can you imagine it? I just left them in the garden because they told me the interrogation wouldn't take long."

Yes, I thought when I spent the second night in the cell without Nur. She is probably already reunited with her children; she has survived this hell. And I should be happy and content that I would never see my friend again.

However, just as I started to make peace with this thought, they brought Nur back. Two guards opened the cell door and threw her straight onto the floor. She looked awful; her entire face was splotchy, and her blue prison uniform was saturated in both dried and fresh blood. Even her hair was sticky with blood. She had been tortured in the worst way imaginable. The security people must have believed they could force information about her brother in Afghanistan out of her this way.

Nur remained crumpled on the floor because she didn't have the strength to stand up again. She was simply too weak to do so. And none of us were allowed to help her or to even speak with her. I will never forget the expression in her eyes as she looked up at me from below. Her eyes filled with tears, but I could do nothing for her. I could only gaze at her, and that broke my heart.

After some time, we helped Nur at least to sit up. Then, as usual, we were instructed over the loudspeaker about what to do next. She tried gradually to once again participate in the collective activities in our cell, but it was hard for her because she was too physically weakened to do so.

At ten o'clock, when we received the order to go to sleep, we agreed that she should be allowed to stretch out on the floor and rest first. I stood beside her. After several hours, the time to switch came, but I offered to stand through the night so she could rest longer. "You should keep resting," I whispered.

But Nur refused. "I'm okay," she claimed. And so we changed places; I lay down, and Nur took her place among the other women. To this day, I wish I hadn't let her do that.

At some point in the night, I heard a loud thud. I immediately knew what had happened: Nur had collapsed. She had toppled over and passed out from fatigue and weakness. I rushed over to help her, then heard her exhale very noisily, twice in succession. These were tremendously deep, eerie-sounding breaths that seemed to come from the deepest part of herself. She was exhaling the last of her remaining life energy.

I intuitively grasped that she had died. "Nur is dead!" I screamed.

"Silence, Number 17!" came the prompt reply from the loud-speaker.

At first, I thought our guards would leave her there and ignore me, but the cameras had recorded what had happened, and our watchers on the other side realized what had happened. Two guards entered our cell a few minutes later and went to Nur. One raised her right arm, felt her pulse, and confirmed my suspicion. "Number 23 is dead," he declared.

The women standing around us sighed audibly. Some started biting their hands again to keep from sobbing out loud. Aygul, as usual, was the only one to give voice to her frantic thoughts. "Lucky woman, she's released from this hell! But we'll all get out of here eventually, too, either dead or alive," she exclaimed. "The only question is, which of us will be next?"

"Shut up!" the guards hissed.

But she ignored them. "You assholes will get your punishment soon," she promised them, unperturbed.

With that, the guards left us, although they didn't take Nur. Her body was still lying where she had collapsed in the midst of us in that hopelessly crowded room. Via the loudspeaker, we were ordered to cross our arms behind our heads and to turn to face the walls with our eyes fixed on the floor. Despite that, I watched what happened next out of the corners of my eyes.

Several figures in black uniforms entered the room. They were members of the police special forces, and their faces were concealed behind dark masks. This distinguished them from the normal camp guards, who wore khaki uniforms and showed us their faces. However, the special forces were responsible for disposing of bodies, and obviously, the masks were an attempt to ensure we couldn't identify them. Rumor had it that they never took off the masks or showed their faces to each other. The authorities were at least a little nervous about the possibility that all the crimes they committed inside the camps might come to light one day.

The masked officers brought large pliers to grab Nur by the foot. They then dragged her behind them out of the cell like a slab of meat.

I was completely traumatized after this experience. During my incarceration, I witnessed nine such deaths in our cell, but after the death of my friend, I lost my will to live. I no longer saw the purpose behind anything. What was the point of torturing myself if this was how everything would end anyway?

Aygul was right; death was a form of release. It was a release for Nur and would also be a release for me. I knew I couldn't withstand the hardships here much longer. So, like a robot, I did everything they asked of me – and waited to meet the same fate as Nur.

I didn't have very long to wait. Three days after losing my friend, I collapsed on June 9, 2017. After less than two months inside the camp, they carried my unconscious body out of the cell.

CHAPTER 8

Watched Every Step of the Way

I woke up in a bright room and found myself lying on a bed covered with a white sheet. The room smelled of disinfectant. I blinked. A woman in a nurse's coat was arranging medicines on my night-stand—lots and lots of pills. I was in a hospital ward. When I tried to move, I discovered that one of my hands was cuffed to the bed.

I looked down at myself; I was dressed in a white shirt and had shackles on my feet. "She's slowly waking up," I heard the nurse say. She wasn't wearing a uniform, I realized before drifting off again.

When I woke up the next time, a doctor sat at my bedside. She was watching me with kind, brown eyes. "How are you feeling?" she asked me in Uyghur.

It struck me as almost unreal. It had been ages since anyone had asked about how I was feeling. "Thank you, alright," I replied.

"Are you in pain?"

I hesitated before answering. Did she want to help me? In the camp, I learned that even the doctors couldn't be trusted. However, she didn't strike me as a camp doctor. Instead, her smile encouraged me, so I said, "Yes, there." I pointed at my stomach with my free hand.

She didn't look surprised. "You've been ingesting too many drugs," she confided in a subdued tone. "Try not to take any more of them for a while." I nodded, although I didn't exactly understand what she was trying to tell me. "If you can drink a lot of milk, that should also help to cleanse your system…."

"Okay," I said, relaxing a little. I could tell that the woman had my best interests at heart. "Thank you." I hardly dared to ask when I had to return to my cell.

"You need to rest for now. At least until you're back on your feet again, you'll stay home with your parents."

"Really?!" I could hardly believe my good luck. Even one day at home would be a joyous occasion because I could at least see my children again. I had given up hope of that ever happening again.

I was released one day later. A police vehicle initially transported me from the hospital to the police station. I was scared they would lock me up again, but nothing like that happened. Instead, an officer instructed me to behave in the "free world." "You are forbidden to tell anyone about what you experienced during your training," she declared emphatically. *Training* was a euphemism for the *camp*, slowly making inroads into our normal language. "Do you understand?" I nodded.

She gave me a wig with shoulder-length dark brown hair to conceal my yet-bald head. "You will wear this from now on," she instructed me. I promised everything she wanted to hear. "What has become of you? Do your parents deserve such a child who has broken the law?" These sentences that I had repeated so often now echoed in my ears. And I was wildly determined not to cause my parents any more worries. I would be a good daughter and a good citizen from now on.

Before I could leave, two Chinese officers were appointed to accompany me home. They weren't wearing any uniforms, but they were obviously plainclothes officers. "These are your new relatives, your beloved brothers from the Chinese motherland," the first officer explained.

One of the songs we had sung in the cell immediately started to play in my head again: "Red, five-starred flags flutter in the wind, as the triumphal song sounds bright and clear. We are singing for our dear motherland; from now on, we will strive toward prosperity and strength…." But what she said confused me. My relatives? What did she mean by that?

"They will reside with you and your family from now on," the officer clarified. "So treat your relatives well."

"Of course," I promised.

"Our eyes and ears see everything," she reminded me, although that was completely superfluous. Nobody knew that better than I did.

I then stood in front of our apartment with the two men. My father opened the door; he didn't look all that surprised. He had received a call from the police informing him of my arrival – or, better said, of our arrival. In any case, he didn't protest about the two men who entered our apartment behind me.

It was an extremely strange situation. More than anything, I wanted to hug my father after our long separation. I wished to weep with him and tell him everything that had happened to me since the police had taken me from our apartment. But instead, I remained silent, and he didn't ask any questions. He didn't ask even once where I had been the whole time, as if it was the most normal thing in the world for someone to be gone for two months.

My aunt didn't say anything, either. She only bit her fingers when she saw me to hold back her tears. "Mihrigul, I hope you're doing well," she said stiffly.

"Yes, mother," I replied just as neutrally. "Where are the children?"

"Elena! Moez!" she called.

The little ones had dashed off when we first arrived. They were two years old now, though still quite shy because they hadn't had many good experiences with strangers. They now peered cautiously out of the bedroom. My heart leaped with joy as I caught sight of my daughter with her tousled curls and my son with yet-his oversized head and his father's darkly glowing eyes.

Spreading my arms out, I automatically expected them to run to me. Instead, they hung back in the doorway and gazed uncertainly at my aunt. "Go on, you two!" she urged them. "Come here and tell your mother hello!" They hesitantly came out of hiding.

"Mama?" Moez asked as I hugged him. He didn't seem to know what to make of all this rightly. Then I started to cry.

"Yes, I'm your Mama," I assured him.

"Mama's coming back soon," Elena claimed.

"Mama's back now," I corrected her. First, she looked at me suspiciously. Then, as I tried to kiss her, she turned away and started to cry.

"I'm your mama," I assured her again, but that didn't help.

"Mama's coming back soon," she repeated stubbornly.

That hurt me deeply. Of course, I tried not to take her rejection personally since I knew my children were overwhelmed by the situation. They had been too small at the time of my arrest to recognize me right away. Nonetheless, I blamed myself terribly for the fact that things had gotten this far.

"Mama will never go away again," I declared, although I had no idea if I could keep this promise. It was just something I wanted to say at the moment because it was my only wish: never to be separated from my children again and to be able to watch them grow up in peace and quiet.

The two Chinese officers moved in with us. They did act like relatives who wanted to stay with my parents and me. However, they didn't behave like loving relatives that someone would be glad to have come to visit, but rather pesky ones, always intruding. They participated in our day-to-day activities without being asked. For example, when we ate our meals, they joined us at the table and demanded to be served, which was difficult because we hardly had enough for ourselves. And when I played with my children, they watched over my shoulder. They went everywhere in our apartment, even into our bedrooms. And they didn't settle in temporarily with us, but permanently.

We were initially baffled by this new concept. Of course, this wasn't the first time security officers had been in our apartment, but the previous officers had always worn uniforms and projected themselves as intruders. These so-called "relatives," however, denied us any sense of distance.

On the first evening they were there when it was about time for everyone to go to bed, my father said that he would prepare a place for them to sleep in the living room, as he would have also done for relatives. But the men protested. "We won't be sleeping in the living room but in your bedroom," they declared. Therefore, my father began to prepare one of the two rooms for them, each containing a bed; in our case, this consisted of a wooden bedframe and a large rug covering the frame. My parents typically slept in one of these beds, while the children and I slept in the other. However, the Chinese officers weren't satisfied with their separate quarters. "But we're your dear relatives; we will sleep in the beds with you," they explained.

The men insisted on dividing up so each could sleep in one of the beds. My father flushed darkly when he heard this. As a Muslim man, even the thought of my aunt or I sharing a bed with strange men was deeply demeaning and shameful. Under normal circumstances, he would have kicked them out of our home or beaten them up for even making such a brazen suggestion. In this case, though, he tried to keep himself under control as he attempted to devise a solution that would be the least damaging to all of us. He needed to prevent either of us women from having to share a bed solo with one of these men. In the end, we all slept together: my aunt, the two children, the Chinese officer, and I. My father shared the bed in the other room with the second officer.

To prevent any personal relationships from developing between the Chinese men and us, the men were swapped out every other week. However, all the "visitors" who stayed with us were rude individuals without any manners whatsoever. I suspect these were random good-for-nothings out of China who were not gainfully employed in their hometowns yet gleefully lorded it over us at every turn. Their jobs now obviously consisted exclusively of terrorizing us and behaving so badly that we no longer felt at home within our own four walls. Unfortunately, my family wasn't the only one subjected to such treatment. It was a widespread campaign; one out of ten Uyghur families had Chinese "relatives" move in with them and take over their family's private life. Outside of the prison walls, this was the ultimate assault against us in 2017 and 2018.

In principle, all of Xinjiang was functioning like a prison camp. Or better said: With these "visitors," it didn't make any difference if you were inside or outside a camp. Their presence within families made the surveillance and dehumanization on both sides of the barbed wire complete. Even in our most private spaces, in our Uyghur bedrooms, there was no escape from Chinese state violence.

In our neighborhood, we were treated like pariahs. Our neighbors, as well as our more distant family members, avoided us and never voluntarily spoke to us. Clearly, they could bring harm to themselves if the authorities registered any connection between us. We also stopped talking to each other, despite the fact that I had always discussed things with my parents. During the years I studied in China and Egypt, I called them frequently to tell them what was going on with me and ask their opinions. This no longer occurred. The children were the only ones with whom we still exchanged a few unselfconscious words. We, adults, limited ourselves to communicating through glances, but the men closely monitored even that.

Our Chinese "relatives" were constantly jotting down notes. For example, if I exchanged a meaningful look with my father, they instantly scribbled something in their books. Once a day, they took these books to the police station to file reports on us. Of course, they might have also received new instructions at those times. Regardless, they naturally never went to the station at the same time since that would have entailed leaving us at home, alone and unwatched.

Our family life, including our relationships with each other, suffered horribly under this strain. For me, it was especially awful to see my father so manipulated and powerless. As a child and as I grew older, I had always viewed him as a strong man. Even in prison, I had treasured this image, clinging to the hope that my father would somehow manage to get me out. But now I could see he was just as helpless as I was. And that unsettled me. I didn't want this marionette but the strong father that I loved so much. That was why I increasingly ignored him; he was still physically present but wasn't the person I knew.

And so my loneliness grew – it increased for all of us. We perceived the other people as pictures of the individuals they had once been, like misleading packaging that looked just the same but had been filled with different contents.

To admit this to myself was quite painful. Although my parents were seemingly still with me, there was no one I could confide in. Instead, I was forced to maintain a facade everywhere I went constantly. Even in front of my children, I had to play a role to keep from upsetting them. For their eyes, I pretended the strange circumstances we were living in were completely normal. Whenever I gave them something to eat or played with them, I tried to act happy for their sake.

The bathroom was the only place in the apartment where I could relax and be myself. Nobody followed me inside there, and I could cry. I often retreated behind the bathroom door to do just that. I sometimes even toyed with the idea of using those unobserved moments to say prayers, but I always wondered if there was a chance they had installed cameras or bugs in the bathroom as well. I never wanted to take that risk.

Besides, I no longer needed a formalized prayer ritual. During my time in prison, I had learned to get by without murmuring surahs or bowing toward Mecca. I could now speak with my God anywhere, at any time. My relationship with Him was stronger than before because it was the only thing I could rely on. Even if everything else was taken away from the people I loved the most behaved like puppets of the Chinese and me, I could always reach Allah, and He was always there for me.

However, I spent most of my time playing a cat-and-mouse game inside our apartment with the men, who followed me everywhere. Of course, they had to write their reports, and there wasn't much for them to report on when it came to us. A life with two small children isn't anything spectacular, which is why the men often got bored.

Whenever my father wasn't around, the men would harass my aunt and me. One guy, who was quite fat, would always stalk me from behind. For example, he followed me when I stepped into the kitchen one day to fix the children's food. He wrapped his flabby, cheesy arms around me when I opened the refrigerator. I found this revolting and hissed at him that he had to stop doing that. "Take your hands off of me, or I'll tell your boss," I threatened him.

That just seemed to amuse him. As he laughed, I was forced to inhale his foul-smelling breath since he was standing too close to me. "Go ahead and try that," he chuckled. "Do you think you can do anything to me? You think too highly of yourself, girl. Nothing will happen to me."

"We'll see about that!"

"Don't push your luck," he warned me. "Or do you want me to take you back to prison?"

At that moment, my children came into the kitchen – and I was immediately intimidated by his unvarnished threats. This man was more powerful than I was, and I shouldn't antagonize him. But how was I supposed to protect myself against him?

"Just don't touch me. I have a contagious disease," I eventually claimed.

But even that didn't impress him; his brashness increased. When I found myself alone with him the following day, he ran his hands under my dress and fondled my breasts.

Nonetheless, the worst were the nights with him. At first, the man slept next to my father, but then the two officers swapped places, and he then slept beside my aunt and me. We had decided long before this to go to bed in our regular clothes so we didn't have to undress in the evenings in front of our visitor. The children were the only ones we let dress in pajamas. After that, we would take our positions; my aunt would lie down against the wall, then I stretched out next to her with the children on my other side, and then the stranger. That first night, I lay awake for a long time because I had a bad feeling. At some point, though, I dozed off, only to wake up to the feeling of the man's hand in my hair. I jolted upright in fright. "Stop that right now!" I hissed at him quietly to keep from waking the children.

"Then come out with me."

"No way! I'll scream for help if you do anything to me."

"What would your children think if you did that?"

At moments like that, I sometimes wished I could return to the prison, where at least at night, we women were left alone. I'm still ashamed even to express these things, but they are the truth, which is why I need to put them into words.

I despised that man with every pore of my body and wished I could kill him. Longingly, I waited for him to be replaced, but the days dragged on.

After a few more sleepless nights next to him, my murder plans grew more concrete. I considered where I could scrounge up a knife to slit his throat. Regardless of the consequences, I would cut his throat if he touched me again. At least, that was what I imagined doing whenever I felt brave and strong. On the weaker days, when I was overcome with despair, I wished to end my own life, not his. Either way, I needed a knife.

And so I started searching, but there were no knives anywhere. Several months ago, Chinese officers had gone from house to house and confiscated all the knives owned by Uyghur citizens. At the same time, a law had been passed declaring that every household in Xinjiang was limited to owning only two knives: one for cutting meat and one for cutting vegetables. The state distributed these knives, and the authorities knew who owned which one. The knives were stamped with an identification number and furnished with a tracking chip to keep them from going missing. My parents also had two of these knives in their kitchen. The officials had attached them to a chain so they couldn't be used anywhere else in the apartment.

I soon accepted that my knife-themed murder fantasies would never come to fruition because there weren't any knives around. Or maybe I was too cowardly to lure the Chinese officer into the kitchen. Though she paid the price, my neighbor Patime was more courageous than I was.

One night, when I couldn't sleep, I heard a loud banging and yelling from above our heads. It sounded like a fight, and someone screamed. Then, with horror, I recognized the voice of the eight-year-old girl who lived upstairs from us: the daughter of our neighbor Patime.

We had hardly any contact with our neighbor's family. When I returned from the camp, my aunt informed me that the neighbor's husband was in prison. This was why nobody in our building spoke to her. I shouldn't say anything to her, either, if I happened to run into her on the stairwell. "It would be better for us," my aunt declared. "We're already in enough trouble." I knew that. So when a Chinese officer moved in with Patime and her daughter, my parents and I registered this development with a shrug. We felt sorry, though, that Patime and her child had to live with the Chinese man all by themselves, but when the authorities ordered a "familial visitation," there was no point in trying to fight it.

For the past few months, just like us, Patime had had a permanent guest staying in her apartment who changed his face every other week. Her respective "visitor" also shared her bed with her, and we knew the Chinese man would take full advantage of Patime's absent husband. I tried hard not to think about what she was going through, night after night. It had to be much worse than anything I was experiencing. However, that night, the sounds that drifted down to us sounded different.

"Take your hands off of her!" I heard my neighbor scream, followed by another cry from her daughter. It wasn't hard for me to figure out what was happening up there. The man was raping the eight-year-old girl in front of her mother. I shuddered. My aunt also lay stock-still in our bed, listening to the horrifying goings-on.

It was quiet for a while after that, but then there was a renewed crash, and we heard Patime scream. I wanted to hold my ears; he was probably now going after the child's mother. It was excruciating to have to listen to everything. I felt so dreadfully sorry for Patime. She was about the same age as me. I thought about how I would react if I were forced to watch someone hurt my son or my daughter, but I couldn't truly imagine it. I probably would strangle the attacker with my bare hands, even if I died in the process.

I suddenly heard another shout and a groan, but this time it was a masculine voice. I heard a wheezing sound but then nothing else. It all struck me as quite odd. What had just happened in the apartment above us?

Dead silence reigned for the rest of the night. No other sounds made their way down to us from the other apartment. Then, at dawn, police vehicles with sirens came screeching up to our building, and half a dozen officers stormed Patime's apartment. They led our neighbor down the stairs in handcuffs and shoved her into one of the police cars parked in front of our building. They carried her Chinese "relative" down on a stretcher. He was dead. Patime had lured him into her kitchen during the night before ramming the chained-up meat knife into his heart.

We never saw our neighbor again. Rumors circulated in our building that she had tried previously to poison her Chinese roommate or his predecessor, though without success. Soon people heard that Patime had been sentenced to death for the murder. That didn't surprise me. I never learned what happened to her daughter. She had also been led away at the time and probably taken to one of the state "re-education" camps.

Back then, we often heard stories like this. Many Uyghur men threw themselves off the upper floors of apartment buildings because they were forced to watch as Chinese officers raped their wives and daughters. The despair among our people was enormous.

These Chinese "visitors" truly were the worst thing to happen to an Uyghur family because each man behaved more horribly than the one before him. I don't know what the government thought when sending these men to us. Was there a plan behind it? I assume that they hoped this method would drive us out of our apartments and houses. I often heard that the "visitors" remained behind in the homes whenever a family was taken to a camp. This way, the Chinese permanently took over the Uyghurs' homes and replaced them, so to speak. I suspect these so-called "family visitors" were part of a large resettlement program from the Chinese heartland into Xijiang.

Even in the case of my parents' apartment, the Chinese visitors continued to reside there long after we had been removed to the internment camp.

CHAPTER 9

Doomed to Die

In November 2017, I was awakened in the middle of the night by the sound of dogs loudly barking. A bright light blinded me, and my children started screaming. Suddenly four police officers materialized around our bed. I was terrified, but this attack wasn't unexpected. I had suspected it would occur sooner or later; I had only been temporarily released several months before due to my poor health. They were now here to fetch me back.

But I wasn't the only one. In those days, there were mass round-ups of people. Many Uyghurs started sleeping in their street clothes because they lived with the expectation of being picked up during the night. People talked about one well-known Uyghur singer who had sent an encoded post to his fans stating that he lived in constant fear of being arrested. The singer disappeared without a trace in 2018. Most people assume that the Chinese authorities have since arrested him.

Like all the other Uyghur families, we weren't allowed to lock

PLACE OF NO RETURN

our doors so that our home could be entered at any moment. And we also kept our shoes close to our beds, ready to be grabbed. Nonetheless, it was still a shock when our nightmare suddenly turned into reality.

Under my aunt's horrified gaze, the police snapped handcuffs on me. "Stand up, let's go!" they bellowed over the yapping of their dogs. The only thing they couldn't drown out was the hysterical sobbing of my children. Even my aunt lost her semblance of control. "Why do you want to take her?" she cried out sharply. "What has she done?"

"Keep your mouth shut, or we'll take you with us, too," the men said menacingly.

They yanked me out of bed by the handcuffs, and I fell face-first onto the floor. "Stand up immediately!" they shouted, and I picked myself up. I wanted to get this situation behind me as quickly as possible because I couldn't stand the sound of my children sobbing for me. I put up no resistance as they dragged me to the door.

"Stop!" my aunt shouted, running after me. She was holding my boots. "Let her at least put her shoes on! She can't go out without shoes on!"

The men ignored her. They pushed me toward the door as they pulled a sack over my head. "Let's go! We don't have all night!" they declared coldly.

"No, the shoes!" I heard my aunt insist behind me. And as they guided me out of the apartment, I heard her loudly discussing this matter with the men. She even convinced one of them to listen to her. He handed me my shoes after I was loaded into the back of the police van.

"Come on, put them on. That way, you won't catch a cold," he said with equal parts sarcasm and pity.

The officers drove me to the police station and roughly pushed me out of the vehicle. I was so glad to have something on my feet since November was bitterly cold. Our temperatures were below freezing. But despite that fact, the heat wasn't running in most parts of the police station into which they led me.

They locked me up in a cell on the ground floor that was so small that I couldn't even stretch out my arm's full length or move around much at all. There were bars at the front of the cell that let out on the corridor. The floor was composed of cold plastic, and all the walls were covered with gray foam. The reason for this was obvious; many prisoners tried to kill themselves by beating their heads against the walls. The foam prevented them from achieving that goal.

I can't say that I was tired of living myself. I certainly wouldn't have voluntarily ended my life. I think no mother of three-year-olds could bring herself to do that, even if her situation was quite dire. For the children's sake alone, she would find the will to live; in my case, I felt it was an obligation that I bore. Nonetheless, I had lost my optimism. Now that I had been arrested for the third time, I felt strangely numb. It was clear that regardless of what they planned to do to me here, there was nothing I could do to change it. All I could do was bear up under whatever Fate held in store for me.

With this basic attitude, I waited for them to come to get me for interrogation. I thought about my previous interrogations and the pain they inflicted on me. Would they do that again? Would they torture me once more? What in heaven's name did these people think they could squeeze out of me? What law had I broken? They hadn't been able to accuse me of anything from my time in Egypt, despite having written down what I had done for every second I was there. Nor did they have anything on me here in Xinjiang, where they had kept constant surveillance over my entire life.

The longer I thought about it, the more I believed that I had nothing to fear this time. What forbidden thing could a woman do when locked up at home with her two young children? They had to just be trying to intimidate me. They would probably interrogate me and then send me back home. With two Chinese officers as housemates, it hardly made any difference if I were inside or outside a detention center.

I waited and waited, but no one came to interrogate or even talk to me. Since natural light shone through the bars of my cell, I knew that exactly two days had passed. I had spent two long days in this gray foam box, watched the whole time by two cameras. I began to wonder what the officials intended to do. Was this perhaps some new form of torture they had dreamed up for me? And what would follow it? An interrogation? Freedom? A new cell? How long would I be stuck here?

At the end of the third day, the guards finally unlocked the door. It's time; I thought as they pulled another sack over my head and dragged me out of my cell by my handcuffs. They were going to interrogate me now.

They led me into a room, and as they removed the sack, I was blinded by the garish, artificial light. Nonetheless, I could see immediately that several police officers were sitting across from me. Their arrangement reminded me of a tribunal instead of a judge or jury. Only people in uniform were sitting there.

"All Uyghurs living abroad have now been brought back by the Chinese government," the lead interrogator, who was Han Chinese, informed me. I think only one of the officers in the room was Uyghur; all the rest were from outside the province.

"We have interrogated all of these individuals, particularly those who lived in Cairo like you. Everything you did there was closely watched, which is why we now have lots of evidence of your crimes. You won't gain anything by denying what we know. We can prove all the stuff you've done…."

I had no idea what the man was talking about. What crimes did he mean? I hadn't committed any!

"Don't act dumb. Now is the time to confess," he said, staring at me belligerently. But there was nothing I could say because there wasn't a single crime that I could have admitted to.

"Even if you don't think you've done anything wrong, just tell us," he insisted.

"But I haven't done anything," I assured him. "Truly!"

It was obvious that he wasn't satisfied with this. By this point, I'd had enough experience with interrogations to know that. The Chinese officers were never content with my answers; they always sniffed around for some hidden offense. And yet there was nothing else that I could say since I couldn't just concoct something on the spot to make them happy. So I said nothing.

Then he began to insult me. "You know what you did, but you don't want to tell me," the interrogator claimed. And then he grew furious. "All the training we've put you through has been pointless! You are intransigent," he shouted accusingly. "You refuse to admit to your crimes, even though they're more than apparent!"

The other men also started to badger me. "You're ungrateful," they said reproachfully. "You aren't worthy of the love our government has shown you."

They increasingly talked themselves into a rage, and I waited for them to start inflicting physical pain on me. Due to my previous interrogation experiences, I was somewhat prepared for this. But they didn't touch me, which was quite unexpected since they were all wearing police cudgels on their bodies.

It slowly dawned on me that, this time, they were playing a different game with me. This game was almost worse than the physical violence; they wanted to break me psychologically.

"Why should we beat you?" one of them asked. "That would take too much effort. We're done with you. You're already classified in the second most serious criminal category. Either you can confess now, or you'll face the death penalty."

He hesitated as his threat echoed throughout the room while the others concentrated on my reaction. However, I didn't react. Although I should have been afraid, I stayed oddly impassive.

I think this is what happens when you are deadened inside. Over the past few years, the police and camp officers had done so much to me that even the direct threats to my life had lost their terror. Did they want to kill me? That struck me as the logical next step for them to take after everything else they had done. Was I supposed to burst into tears and plead for mercy? No. It was as if a protective glass wall surrounded me, one that cut me off from all emotions.

This seeming indifference antagonized my tormentors even more. "You'll probably be shot." Then, they started to describe what my impending death would be like. "That's why we aren't torturing you anymore. It won't do any good. There's no point in torturing someone who's going to die anyway."

"It really is a pity for a woman like you," one of the other men remarked. "We tried hard with you, but our patience can't last forever."

They made me feel like my sentence was as good as set in stone. "The only way you can stop this from happening is by giving us a full confession," the lead interrogator declared. "Think about it. We will give you some time to consider it." He looked down at me with seeming regret. "It would be a shame for you."

With these words, the interrogation ended, and they had me locked back up again. Two security guards pulled the sack over my head again and led me to a transport van in the yard. "Come on, get in!" they said.

"Where are you taking me?"

Instead of answering, they pushed me roughly into the vehicle. "You'll find out soon enough." With that, they turned on the engine. After a twenty-minute drive, we passed a security checkpoint and entered a secured area. A camp? A prison? It was all the same to me.

When I was admitted, I had to remove my clothes once again. A doctor in uniform examined me and found me sufficiently healthy for detention. My hair was shorn off, and I received new hand and wrist shackles and a new prison uniform, which was no longer blue but orange. "Do you know what that means?" the woman who handed me the clothes inquired, her face reflecting disgust. "That means that you're a serious criminal!"

This orange clothing was like a curse. Everyone who saw me in it knew immediately what was going on with me and to which category of inmates I belonged. The guards, especially, never skipped an opportunity to remind me of that. "You don't have much longer to live," they regularly remarked. "We're just waiting for them to give us your final verdict, and then you're going to die." All my fellow inmates also knew about me, thanks to my clothes.

I was initially spared dealing with the other inmates because I was once again condemned to a solitary cell. The cell was like the previous one: small and cold, with foam-covered walls that swallowed every sound. In there, I felt like I was inside a cotton box. Presumably, they wanted to give me another chance to change my mind and make the confession that the interrogator had demanded of me. But I couldn't produce this, regardless of my isolation. The security officers eventually realized this as well, so after ten days, they moved me to a cell with twenty other women.

All the women in this new cell wore blue prison uniforms. When they caught sight of my orange clothing, they peevishly turned their backs on me. None of them spoke to me, not even a few whispered words in greeting. Instead, they treated me like someone with a serious disease you would want to avoid touching at all costs. They even refused to make eye contact with me. The only thing missing was them turning their noses up when they saw me.

There was only one exception to this. In the farthest corner, I discovered one other woman in orange clothing, who was also wearing foot shackles like me. She was quite tall but extremely thin and haggard. She looked like a walking corpse with her almost transparent skin and deeply shadowed eyes. However, she was the only woman who briefly smiled at me. I later learned that Gulbahar had been waiting for nineteen months for her execution.

She was a pariah, just like me. The rest of the women viewed us as dangerous, or at least any contact with us to be so. After all, cameras were hanging all over the cell that followed our every move. We two "serious criminals" naturally required very close observation, so none of the women risked getting close to us.

The pointed disregard by the rest of the group was a new experience for me. I had found my previous incarcerations to be wretched – but differently. In those instances, it had been the external circumstances that had worn away at us. Our tormentors had been located on the other side of the bars, while those of us on the inside had formed a solidarity with one another. In this cell, there was no solidarity, at least not for Gulbahar and me. We had to be careful of the other women since some were working with the guards. They spied on the two of us to get better food or other advantages, although I don't know if they did this to the others. Regardless, this generated a climate of insecurity, and I felt I couldn't trust anyone.

This was why I was all the more amazed by Gulbahar, who always carried her head high despite her physical state. It was almost as if she were proud of her condition. She had exemplary manners and always remained friendly, even though her cellmates often treated her badly. Once, when a woman snatched away her piece of steamed bread and popped it into her mouth right in front of her, Gulbahar gave her a kind smile.

She was just as serene when it came to the harassment from the guards, who also had it in for her. While all the others were addressed with their assigned numbers, they simply called Gulbahar "Terrorist." "Hey, Terrorist, stand up straight!" they ordered her. Of course, everyone knew who they meant at those times. I felt bad for her, but Gulbahar just smiled and did what they asked of her.

At first, I thought she was a little crazy, but then I understood that this gentleness was part of her character. At some point, she must have decided that she wouldn't change this part of herself, regardless of how horrid those around her behaved. "They aren't bad people. They're just scared," she whispered to me once, thus taking her tormentors under her wing as well. I admired her greatly for this attitude, which helped her rise above those who wanted to harm her. She refused to engage them on their level but maintained her position on a morally higher plane. I found this astonishing.

Unfortunately, I didn't have this graciousness within me. It made me angry whenever the guards used their power against us, or the other women made us feel like criminals of the lowest order. I often despaired over this. Once, when I was sitting on the floor and believed that I was unobserved, tears welled in my eyes. I tried to turn my head so that the camera couldn't see me to avoid the sneering commentary that would otherwise come from the loudspeaker. I hadn't noticed that Gulbahar was sitting next to me.

"Hey, you shouldn't cry," she murmured to me. "You need to hold your head high. We will get through this!" Her voice sounded sweet in my ears. "The Uyghurs living abroad are fighting for this insanity to end soon. You'll see. Our people will be coming before long to free us. Hang in there! Preserve your dignity because they will be here soon...."

Her words comforted me even if I didn't completely believe what she said. At least at one point, Gulbahar was right. We couldn't relinquish our dignity, even if we were helplessly at their mercy. We were the only ones who could destroy our dignity – and we shouldn't let that come to pass. *Yes, I might actually die here*, flashed through my head at that moment, but if that was going to happen, I wanted to go with my head held high. I glanced over at Gulbahar, and she smiled at me encouragingly.

Thinking about her today makes me cry. What became of proud Gulbahar? She was probably sentenced to death and shot. I can't imagine that she is still alive.

The daily routine in this third prison was quite different from that in the first and second camps, where the brainwashing of the prisoners had been the primary goal. That wasn't going on here. We didn't have to busy ourselves with the Red Book, memorize slogans, or sing songs. There were also no marching orders. Instead, this place was more like a detention center for individuals who had been identified as delinquent but whom the authorities were no longer trying to convert.

This mainly translated into our day-to-day lives as boredom. Without the readings and the songs, I had nothing to do all day except sit around and wait on mealtimes. In the mornings, there was rice water, while lunch was stone-hard steamed bread, and supper was just enough cooked rice to keep me alive, barely. I felt starved and weak. The guards made it clear to me: "You're dead anyway. Why should we take any trouble when it comes to you? You'll only be here until your verdict comes through."

But this final sentence took a long time to come. Morning after morning, I woke up expecting that this might be the day on which the die of my fate would be cast. But I kept getting that wrong. I eventually grew so weary of the waiting that I almost wished that the judges – or whoever was making the decision – would hurry up and declare the verdict so that my waiting could come to an end. This uncertainty and the fear that it might all be over, which ran contrary to the hope that kept taking root inside me, proved quite stressful. I just wanted to know if I was going to live or die.

During this period of waiting, I changed cells several times. As the rationale for this, I was repeatedly told that I had to make room for new inmates since the camp was overcrowded. They really wanted to prevent me from forming friendships with the other women, which might have helped me feel more emotionally stable. After all, solidarity is a strong bond that can make even the worst of situations easier to bear.

In each cell, they stuck me; the women had been intimidated before my arrival. The guards had explicitly warned them not to associate with the orange-clad, serious criminal or to even speak to her. Thus, I was met with waves of uncertainty and disapproval regardless of where I found myself. At some point, I accepted the role of pariah and stopped speaking to anyone of my own accord.

However, I was naturally curious about the other women, especially the new ones that regularly showed up. They weren't necessarily coming straight from their homes but had often been transferred from other camps in the region. And when they talked about what they had been through there, I pricked up my ears. This way, I learned a lot about the general state of affairs in Qarqan.

The situation was disastrous by the Spring of 2018. Without exception, every Uyghur family had, by this point, one or more relatives in the camps. In addition, entire extended families were often interned under suspicion.

Roughly speaking, the system functioned like this: The authorities arrested people when there were enough grounds for suspicion, such as, in my case, my time studying abroad and my marriage to an Egyptian. These individuals were interrogated over several days. Then they were stuck in prison, where they were classified as serious or less serious offenders based on the information that had been gathered. The individuals who had committed no grave or at least less grave offenses had to work during their incarceration. They were only brought back to their cells to sleep. During the day, they had to labor in some factory or the other, usually in the clothing industry. Only those considered serious criminals, such as myself were not made to perform forced labor. The reason for that was logical; the authorities were afraid that we would find some way while at the workplace to end our lives. Many people dream of nothing but finding release through suicide.

Once, a woman came to us with terribly rough, chafed hands. "I think this has been caused by the chemicals used in the factory," she told the others.

"Where is that? And what do you make there?" I dared to ask.

And since she was new and the guards hadn't turned her against me yet, she replied.

She explained that she worked in a pastry factory preparing cakes. Every morning at four o'clock, the Chinese security guards covered the eyes of her and other prisoners before driving them into the production halls. After a fifteen-hour shift on the assembly line in the evenings, they returned the prisoners to the camp. "They have hand creme there, but only for the supervisors. We aren't allowed to use any of it," the woman told us.

I even knew one of the other women who joined us. I had been acquainted with Meryem because we came from the same village. Since she was well-to-do, she often gave clothes to children from poorer families, including my grandmother and me. From her, I received a pale blue wool sweater I had worn for several winters.

Meryem had been married to a man fifteen years her senior. He had been wealthy and had given her a car years ago. All the children had admired her whenever she hurtled through our village with it. However, this man, her husband, was also very pious – so he was arrested early on and stuck in a camp. After about a year, he passed away, at which time the police came to arrest her.

Meryem cried as she explained all this, and I wished I could console her. It was on the tip of my tongue to tell her how much I had adored her warm, soft sweater, but I pulled myself together because I could tell that she didn't recognize me or was at least acting as if she didn't recognize me. I didn't want to embarrass her in front of the cameras by drawing attention to her acquaintance with a serious criminal. Perhaps it should remain my or our secret – and my declaration of affection to her.

"Number 54, come forward!" the guards shouted into the cell one morning. I approached the guards with the tiny steps that my foot shackles allowed. Were they about to transfer me to another cell? I had been relocated so often that this no longer surprised me. For months, they had been dragging me all around the camp.

"Your verdict has been handed down," they announced. "You've been given the death penalty."

Although I had frequently imagined this moment during my incarceration, the news struck me as a hard, abrupt blow. The finality of this verdict left no more room for dreams that everything could still take a miraculous turn for the better. My fate was sealed, and I could now stop hoping.

They took me out of my cell and left me in a different one where I had all to myself. The room was relatively nice, at least in comparison to the previous cells. It was even furnished with a narrow cot, a chair, and a small table. In my eyes, this was pure luxury. It felt as if they were unexpectedly lodging me in a hotel room. To top it all off, the guards removed the shackles from my feet; the only thing I had to retain was the handcuffs. "So that you can enjoy your final days," they declared graciously.

"Thank you," I said huskily. All this confused me terribly. I couldn't be happy about the respite I was granted because it made my approaching end all the more tangible and concrete. And I could easily extrapolate what the officers wished to say to me through this special treatment: "We're serious. We are going to kill you."

So that there could be no doubt about what they planned to do to me, they started to go through the details of my execution with me right away. "There are two options for your death," one of the men said. He was Chinese and the higher ranking of the two officers. "You may choose to either be shot or to receive a lethal injection." I stared at him and tried to hide my bewilderment from him. He treated this topic as if presenting me with supper options. I didn't say anything.

"You're probably wondering what the difference is," he continued. "Well, let me explain it to you. The injection would take a little longer than the shooting. This is because you would have to wait until the toxin spreads throughout your body, which differs for each person. For some, a low dose is enough, but others must get a second injection after twenty minutes because the first dose doesn't do the trick. You'll end up writhing in pain, but your heart won't stop beating...."

I nodded but found his commentary unbearable; his words forced me to imagine my own death. Which was, in all likelihood, the intention behind his extensive explanations.

"The shooting wouldn't take as long," the man continued. "We have some very good shooters. Three shots and you're dead. If I were in your shoes, I would pick the shooting option."

"Okay."

"However, it doesn't come for free. Do you have any money?"

"Money?" My first thought was that I had misheard him. "For my execution?"

"Yes. Each shot costs 600 yuan. Of course, you have to pay in advance."

"I understand," I said, shaking my head and feeling nauseous. Was he really suggesting that my family pay for my execution? It had actually come this far. "No, I don't have any money."

"Well, then, the only option is the injection. You'll have to sign a form beforehand agreeing to that. Also, after your demise, your body will belong to the hospital and be released for medical experimentation."

Before leaving me alone, the man promised to bring me the appropriate form shortly. Feeling frustrated, I stretched out on my cot. Was this everything, I wondered. Was my life about to end with a lethal injection? I was only twenty-seven years old and barely began to live. I'd had so many plans after I graduated. I had been so ambitious that I'd moved abroad. And now I was lying here and waiting for my executioner. I couldn't understand how it could have come to this. What had I done wrong?

The Chinese officer and Uyghur guard brought food to my cell that evening. I could tell they were treating me much nicer than usual – as if they felt sorry for me. And the food was better as well. Instead of dry rice, there was now rice sauteed with a little paprika, and it smelled good. My stomach growled as I accepted the plate.

The Uyghur woman, who must have heard that, wished me *bon appetite* before encouraging me to share any particular requests I might have. If there were a special meal I wanted to have one last time before my death, she would try to make it. "Perhaps some lagman (noodle stew) with a little lamb meat?" she suggested.

Tears sprang to my eyes when she said that. I immediately envisioned the delicious, rich noodle soup my grandmother cooked for me. I loved that soup, but the thought of tasting it for the last time was incomprehensible to me.

"Well, just think about it," the woman said. "We want your last days to be good ones."

"How many days do I still have?" I managed to ask.

"I can't tell you that, but not all that many," she said vaguely. "Anyway… if there's anything you still want to get off your chest, you should do that now."

The following day, the same guard returned and brought me a few pieces of paper and a pencil. She smiled at me. "I know you must still have thoughts in your head," she said. "You can write down anything else you want to say. Maybe as a letter to your parents or your children? With your thoughts for posterity, your last words to them."

I suddenly wondered if they would ever receive that letter, but I didn't dare ask that question aloud. "Thank you," was all I mumbled. "That is very nice of you." However, I don't know if it was niceness on her part – or yet another perverse attempt to elicit information from me through clever psychological manipulation.

I stared at the paper and couldn't come up with anything to write at first. My mind was completely blank, like an empty box. I couldn't see past the thought that my life would end. I wasn't ready to die, which was why I was suffering from shock.

However, after some time, my mental state shifted. The more time I spent alone in the death cell, the more questions began to bob around in my head. What would happen to my children after I died? To my parents? Would they be able to take care of my children? Or were they perhaps already in a camp somewhere, too? The question of justice also kept popping up: Why was all this happening? Why did my relatives and I have to suffer so much? How could Allah let something like this happen? What was the point of it?

Then I wept, which I hadn't been able to do before now. I had always kept my composure and hardened myself against my circumstances to survive. But there was no reason to keep that up now. It was alright for me to give up and relax my self-control, so the tears now spilled out of me. I sobbed over all the injustice that had happened to me. But, above all, I regretted the suffering I had brought down on my family. My parents had never deserved for me to cause them so many worries. And as for my children, they needed a strong, protective mother. How badly I wished I could have been that for them, especially for my firstborn! I anxiously wondered if they would ever be able to forgive me.

I knelt on the floor and lowered my head, although I knew without a doubt that the cameras were watching me. It didn't matter anymore, though. "Allah, I don't understand your plan, but I accept my fate," I prayed to my God. "I accept my death, even if I can't see the sense of it. Nonetheless, all humans must die – and you alone determine when that happens. For that reason, I trust in Your wisdom."

After I spoke these words, I slowly began to feel calmer. But there was one final request: "Please let this be enough. Please let me young children live," I begged of God. "Have mercy on them! They are only innocent children. Please protect them, even if I'm not able to." Then, I wondered, would I be admitted to paradise? I had tried to lead a God-fearing life. But regardless of what Allah decided, death and the afterlife couldn't be worse than my earthly existence.

I slept very well during the coming nights. I had fascinating dreams in which I returned to my childhood village. There I saw glorious meadows full of brightly colored wildflowers, and I could fly at night. I can still recall one dream in particular: the sky above me suddenly opened. A ray of light burst through the cloud cover, and a voice said: "Fly!" So I spread out my arms and flew over the lush, green landscape. It was magnificent.

These dreams showed me that I had made my peace with the inevitable. Despite all the injustice, I managed to find inner peace. Thanks to the long hours of sleep and the improved food I was now receiving, I started to recover physically. And slowly, the despair I had been feeling subsided, and my spirits returned.

They even came back in full force. For the past three days, I had even started to wish to live again. And so I began to discuss this with God. "Allah, I prayed for you to protect my children, but now I'm asking you to let me do that myself," I prayed. While I uttered these words, I reflected on the fact that my wish was quite brazen. I believed in a God who guided fate, and now I was demanding nothing less than for him to alter his plans for me. I didn't change course on this, though: "Allah, please let me be the one to care for my children," I begged desperately. "Please give me back my life!"

I didn't hold any real hope that anything would be changed by this, though. And when the guards arrived the next morning, I was prepared for the worst.

CHAPTER 10

Salvation

The guards were in a bad mood. Two days before this, they had started treating me disrespectfully once again. They hurled insults at me and stopped bringing me decent food. I didn't know what that meant, but I suspected nothing good when they pulled another awful black sack over my head, just like all the others I had worn so often. Where could they be taking me this time in the darkness of this fabric? Wasn't everything over where I was concerned? Was I now being taken on my final journey?

Flanking me on either side, the guards led me down the long corridors of the camp. I knew the two of them; they were the man who had brought me my food and the woman who had occasionally accompanied him and urged me to write down my final thoughts. However, the sheets of paper and the pencil remained untouched on the table. Were they going to torture me now to extract some last bit of information? Or were they now going to make speedy work of me? I wished for that for it all to go fast.

Anything, just not the inquisition again. The officers were supposed to give me a quick injection so I could finally find peace
apart from them.

The officers led me into the yard and loaded me into a van. They
were probably taking me to the hospital, where they would give me
the lethal injection and harvest my organs. After everything that
had happened, after everything I had suffered, I was suddenly no
longer afraid. A leaden, eternal weariness spread throughout my
body, and I only wanted it to be quickly over.

After about fifteen minutes of driving, we came to a stop. I had
to get out of the van and walk with the guards into a building that
didn't smell like a hospital. When they removed the sack from my
head, I found myself in a room that looked like an office. On the
table were the jeans, leather jacket, warm boots in which I had
been arrested, and a t-shirt that belonged to my aunt. I looked at
the Uyghur guard questioningly.

"Well, go on, get dressed," she said as she unlocked my handcuffs so I could do that. I didn't understand the rationale behind
this procedure. Why should I wear my personal clothes when receiving the lethal injection?

With a neutral expression on her face, the guard watched me
until I was completely clothed. She then ordered me to sit down in
a chair. "Turn your face toward me," she said, and I saw that she
was fiddling with a container of skin creme and several makeup
items. What was she up to? "I'm going to pretty you up a little,"
she announced.

I had been ready for anything except cosmetic treatment from
a police officer. At first, I thought she was making fun of me or
maybe playing another mind game with me. But when she reached
her fingers into the jar of lotion, I couldn't help laughing. "What
are you doing?" I asked. "Why do you want to pretty me up?"

"Just hold still!" she hissed as she spread the cream on my face.

"Am I supposed to be pretty as I die?"

"No, you're not going to die," she said before ordering me to close my mouth so she could apply lipstick without incident. "Your husband is here."

I didn't believe a single word she was saying anymore. "Why are you making fun of me?"

"You're being released," she insisted. "He's here to pick you up."

I instantly felt my heart start to race as she uttered these words. Okay, Mihrigul, stay calm, I told myself. They're probably joking around at your expense. They're probably playing another of their little games with you. You already know how this goes. After all, what she'd just said *couldn't* actually be true.

The Uyghur woman finished putting on my makeup and then combed my hair, which had started to grow again after four months in prison. She then packed her cosmetic tools into a box and handed me a mirror. The woman who gazed back out at me had plenty of color on her face, though her cheeks were sunken and her eyes were dull. She was wearing my clothes, but I didn't recognize her.

I was still convinced that they were teasing me. Despite that, I couldn't hold back the hope that suddenly flared inside me. The thought that Mahmud could get me out of this hell was too wonderful. Against my will, I glanced toward the door. "He'll be here in just a moment," the guard claimed. And then the door did swing open. Mahmud stepped into the room, accompanied by two police officers. I thought I was dreaming.

My husband looked stunningly handsome. He was wearing a nice dark blue suit and a tie. Although he normally wore a beard, he was clean-shaven and smelled like aftershave. I hardly recognized him. Above all, however, I was deeply ashamed that I had to present myself to him in my condition. More than anything, I wished I could turn invisible. I knew that I looked like a badly made-up zombie, and after several months in prison, I had to stink like a landfill. So I lowered my eyes shyly.

"Mihrigul!" Mahmud said, taking a step toward me.

But I remained rooted where I stood. I wasn't in any mental state to reply to his greeting.

"Don't you know me anymore?" he asked. "It's me, your husband." He gently placed his hands on my shoulders. At that moment, I knew that a miracle had occurred: Allah had heard my prayers. I began to weep softly.

Mahmud wrapped his arms around me. "Don't be scared," he said. "I'm with you again. Everything will be alright now." He was also crying. "I've been so worried about you and the children."

One of the officers interrupted us. "I will now go get the children," he announced before vanishing into another room. I was suddenly overcome by the suspicion that everything I was now experiencing was just a figment of my imagination. Mahmud might evaporate into thin air at any moment. That I was going to now see my children, on top of everything else, was beyond the limits of my comprehension. And yet the officer returned with the two three-year-olds.

I was shocked at their appearance. The children were just as bald as I had been a few months before. Moez had a wound on his chin and a bruise on his forehead. The two of them were filthy as well. Dirt had collected underneath their much-too-long finger and toenails. Their clothes were also torn and dirty. They looked threadbare as if the children had worn only these sets of clothes for weeks and weeks – and they stank horribly, too.

"Moez, Elena!" I cried. I spread out my arms and expected them to run to me, but the boy with the oversized head and the little girl with crossed eyes only looked at me. They seemed unsure if they should come to me or not. That hurt me, but I understood they had just come from a detention camp. It wasn't their fault that they couldn't recognize their mother.

Mahmud stared at the two of them, horror was written all across his face. "Are these really our children?" he asked me. Since he had only seen them when they were infants, he had no recollection of Moez having such a large head or Elena having crossed eyes.

"Yes, this is them."

"But we have three children!"

"This is Moez and Elena," I assured him before falling silent. How often I had imagined this moment when I would have to tell Mahmud about what had happened to our firstborn. But now I had no idea what to say to him.

"And Mohammed?"

"He... is no longer alive."

Mahmud was completely overwhelmed. On the one hand, he was glad to see the two little ones and me. But, on the other hand, he had just learned, without any forewarning, that his oldest son had passed away. He stared into space for a while, attempting to process the information and cope with his conflicting emotions. A sob then escaped him. "How did Mohammed die?" he asked.

"I don't know. They told me he died in the hospital."

"In English, please!" one of the officers shouted. "None of us can speak Arabic here!"

Mahmud ignored him. "You weren't there?" he asked me.

"No," I admitted to him. "I was in prison. They just handed me his body...."

Tears welled up in my eyes, and I couldn't continue talking. He nodded and made no reproach. Nonetheless, I can hardly describe how abysmally wretched and guilty I felt.

While talking, the two children had watched us curiously, though guardedly. "Come, greet your father!" I urged them. I said this in Chinese to appease the officers, who looked quite put out since we ignored their instructions.

The children didn't react. Although they understood my words, they didn't understand what they meant. They hadn't known any father before now. The only man in our family was my father, whom we called the Uyghur word for Grandpa.

Mahmud leaned down to the children and opened a bag he had brought. "Look at what I have here," he said as he pulled out a doll for Elena and two toy cars for our boy. "This is for you!"

The siblings cautiously approached him and first eyed the toys and then the man who had brought them. "Do you even know who I am?" Mahmud asked them. "I'm your father, your *Baba*." Mahmud used the Arabic term of endearment for *father* that he had whispered in their ears when they were babies. The children cocked their heads.

"We don't speak Arabic here!" interrupted the policeman, who had already rebuked Mahmud previously. "You are supposed to speak English here. How often do I have to tell you that?"

"I will speak to my children however I please!" Mahmud snarled in return.

He was on the verge of exploding, and this worried me. Over the past three years, I'd had too many awful experiences with police officers. It would never have occurred to me to challenge them or question their authority. However, Mahmud was made of different stuff; he saw no reason whatsoever to pander to them.

"Enough of this circus!" he snapped at the officer. "You have nothing to say to me." The officer's jaw literally dropped since he was unaccustomed to being spoken to like that. I considered asking Mahmud to tone things down a little, but I didn't want to contradict him in any way.

"We will be going now," he declared, shooting the officer a hostile look.

"Go ahead! Get lost!" the officer replied, gesturing at the door.

"With my wife and children!"

"You may take your children, but your wife will stay with us."

My heart sank. All at once, I realized what was happening here: They just wanted to show me off to Mahmud and lock me back up again. They probably intended to convince him that his wife was still alive so that he couldn't claim anything differently after his return to Egypt. That had been their cruel, devious plan for me all along. They had never taken my release into serious consideration. I felt horribly deceived when I realized this charade. It was as if someone had cleared the entire set of a stage in the middle of a performance.

"Your wife is a Chinese citizen," I heard the officer declare loftily, "so she isn't going anywhere. She has been convicted for her offenses and belongs behind bars, but you may have your children. They are Egyptian citizens. You should be grateful that we fed them for as long as we did. And now get out of here! Go!"

Mahmud's face turned to stone as he realized the dirty game the officers were playing with us. He didn't move an inch and gazed at me pityingly as if he wanted to ask how I had survived so long in the face of such evil.

As for me, I was a step ahead of him already. "Don't worry about me," I whispered. "I'll stay here." After all, I had already made peace with my life. It was a huge consolation to see Mahmud one last time and know that my children were now safe. It was much more than I had dared to hope for when I had repeatedly implored Allah for help. I could now die in peace.

"Take the two children and go!" I urged Mahmud. "Save them! Don't think about me anymore."

But Mahmud refused to listen. "We will only go if we're all together!" he shouted at the officers. "There is no way I'll leave my wife here!"

"You don't have a choice because we just happen not to be in Egypt but in China," the officer reminded him grimly. "Our laws are the valid ones here!"

That finally pushed Mahmud off the deep end. He grabbed the man by the collar and choked him with his bare hands. "You will let my children and wife go this instant!" he shouted. At that moment, the two other officers pulled their guns on him.

Terrified, I begged my husband, "Please let him go, or they'll shoot you." At that, Mahmud lowered his arms. I assumed they would immediately arrest him and lead him away, but instead, the door swung open, and a smartly dressed man with Arabic features stepped inside. It was one of the staff from the Egyptian Embassy, and the chief of the police station trailed him.

"What is going on?" the Egyptian man asked. "Do we have a problem here? Ah, here are the children...."

He spoke in English, though he was quite obviously directing his words at Mahmud. Nonetheless, the two officers felt as if he were speaking to them. Then, to my surprise, they suddenly started acting as meekly as lambs. "Everything is just fine," they declared. "Here are the children. He can take them right now."

The embassy official nodded but only seemed partially satisfied. He shot a questioning glance at Mahmud.

"We were just arguing," my husband said. "They don't want to release my wife, but I won't leave without Mihrigul!" His face reflected his unwillingness to yield on this.

"We will need to discuss this," the Egyptian official turned to face the police chief. "We agreed that Ms. Tursun would also be discharged."

"But of course," the Chinese chief confirmed, shooting his subordinates a scathing glance. "She will be given her discharge papers immediately. As of this moment, Mihrigul Tursun is no longer a Chinese citizen."

With those words, I was set free. I could hardly believe it! Just that morning, I had made my peace with my end, and now I was being released. With my husband and both of my children? It was incredible. I felt relief spread through me, and my legs almost buckled underneath me. It was as if a curse had been lifted from me. The officers had said that I could go wherever I wanted. And the embassy official, Mr. at-Taberi, immediately booked flights for us, first to Ürümqi and then to Beijing.

Although I couldn't wait to leave, I had to see my parents one last time. So I asked the officers for permission to go to our apartment. Naturally, they weren't thrilled at this idea. And so I claimed that I needed to pick up a few personal items there: some clothes, toys for the children, Pampers, etcetera. I'm certain that under normal circumstances, they would have denied me this, but they didn't want to cause any waves with Mr. at-Taberi, the official embassy representative. Thus, I was granted permission, although only with a police escort.

As we sat together in the car and stopped in front of my parents' building, I wondered how I would find them. I hadn't heard anything from them since my arrest. I hoped that the Chinese "relatives" had at least moved out by now. I entered the building in the company of two officers while Mahmud and Mr. at-Taberi remained in the vehicle. The door to our apartment was unlocked, which didn't surprise me since the police had forbidden all Uyghur families from locking their doors. I turned the knob, but as I stepped into the apartment, I could immediately tell something was wrong.

The first thing I noticed was all the dirt that had settled everywhere. That was very unusual since my aunt and I had always placed a lot of emphasis on cleanliness. However, the apartment had not been cleaned in a long time. Besides that, the smell of cold cigarette smoke floated in the air.

I walked through the rooms. In the living room, I came across several ashtrays filled with burnt cigarette butts. Since my parents didn't smoke, I assumed these had come from Chinese men. I also found some pallet beds in there. The two bedrooms, on the other hand, were deserted. There was no trace of my parents.

On the kitchen stovetop stood a pot where my aunt had been preparing soup. The inside of it was covered with mold. Next to it, on a cutting board, I found tiny pieces of rotten Chinese cabbage, tomatoes, and onions, which she had probably chopped up for the soup. However, she had never gotten around to adding them. What had happened here?

I knew only one explanation: my parents had also been arrested. Presumably, the police had taken them by surprise, which was why they had left everything behind. And the Chinese "relatives" had probably stayed longer in our living room. At least, that was how I interpreted the clues I saw.

I was devastated. My poor parents, I thought. How long ago had they been arrested? Where were they now? How were they doing? The thin layer of dust across all the furniture and even the kitchen indicated that several weeks must have passed since their arrest, but it could have been longer, too. My heart tightened. My parents didn't deserve to suffer something like this. Wasn't it enough that the authorities had stuck my children and me in a camp? What had my parents done except support their daughter and grandchildren? What governmental purpose did these mass deportations serve?

"Let's get a move on now," the female officer tore me out of my thoughts. "You wanted to pick up some things...."

"Yes, right."

Although it had only been a pretext, I fished a plastic bag out of a drawer in our kitchen cupboard to hold a few things. As I did that, my eyes again fell on the cutting board with the rotten vegetables and the tea canister behind it. I narrowed my eyes as I noticed something glittering beside the canister.

Oh my God! I needed a moment to grasp what I was seeing. It was my aunt's gold wedding band. She had either taken it off to cut the vegetables or deposited it there because the police had already entered the apartment, and she had wanted to keep the ring safe. I thought the latter was more likely, considering everyone knew that jewelry tended to disappear in police custody.

I absolutely had to take that ring with me, but the officer was standing right behind me, so I quickly turned my head to keep from attracting attention to my discovery. I then walked into my former bedroom, and she followed me. Under her watchful gaze, I collected a pair of pants, a couple of t-shirts, some children's clothes, and powder and diapers from the wardrobe. I stuffed all these things into the bag before explaining that I needed to return to the kitchen to get powdered milk. "Just make it fast!" the officer urged.

I was relieved that she didn't follow me but instead opted to stop and chat with her colleague while I went back into the kitchen. I grabbed the ring and swiftly stuffed it into my pants pocket. I then opened all the kitchen cabinets and pretended to search for powdered milk.

"How long will this take?" the female officer asked as she joined me.

"I can't find the powdered milk...."

"Well, you're just out of luck!" she said. "We're leaving now."

I tried to look disappointed, but inside I was delighted that I had gotten away with my trick without anyone noticing. At least I now had a memento of my parents in case I never saw them again.

We remained in Qarqan for almost two more days, waiting on our flight. During that time, we stayed at the police station. That was our only option since I no longer had a passport, and without valid papers, no hotel in the city would accept me as a guest.

It took a while for me to fully comprehend this dimension of my new status as a stateless person. I was free, but I was something like a fugitive. The authorities now treated me like a foreigner, though one who had no valid papers. I remain convinced that they would have rearrested me if Mahmud and Mr. at-Taberi hadn't always watched over me.

When we went to the airport, no fewer than eight police officers accompanied us. One police vehicle drove in front of us, and another took up the rear. I was very tense and couldn't stop wringing Mahmud's hand because I was scared they would force us to turn back around. I could feel how fearful and distrustful I had become as a result of my three camp detentions. I didn't trust anyone or anything by this point.

We had hardly stepped into the airport terminal when the security personnel intercepted us and moved us into a separate room. I broke out in a nervous sweat. "Let's just go," I implored Mahmud.

"Don't be afraid. They want to take photos of us."

"And what if it's a trap?"

"Everything will be fine," he assured me.

Mahmud took my hand and, gently pressing it, compelled me to come with him. Mr. at-Taberi also encouraged me along. And the personnel did want to take photos of us: first of Mahmud, then of me, and each child individually, followed by several group photos. They then let us go to the boarding gate. A short time later, we boarded the plane to Ürümqi and finally took off.

We reached Beijing after a long, strenuous day of travel. There, too, we encountered the same problem of no hotel wanting to rent us a room. Therefore, the ambassador turned a blind eye and let us spend the night in his guest house. An embassy car picked us up from the airport and took us straight to the property hidden behind a tall wall in the middle of the city. I was relieved when we passed through the barred gate; we were now located on Egyptian territory.

As I sank back into the fragrant, white pillows next to Mahmud and we listened to the exhausted breathing of the twins in the crib next to us, I could hardly contain my happiness. Everything that ordinary people would consider "normal" felt like an unreal luxury, like a gift I had never thought I would receive.

"You saved me," I whispered in Mahmud's ear. "I never thought you would come."

"But of course! I spent the whole time trying to get to you."

My husband told me he had started looking for us when he returned to Egypt. "When I couldn't get through to you, I started to get worried," he explained. "I knew something was wrong, so I immediately applied for another entry visa." A conversation with some international human rights activists about the situation in Xinjiang confirmed his unease.

After that, Mahmud kept returning to the Chinese Embassy, hoping to gain permission to return to China. He planned to fly to Beijing and then travel by land to Xinjiang if he was forbidden from taking other flights. However, the Chinese Embassy in Cairo turned him away repeatedly. Even the fact that his children were located in China did nothing to soften the diplomats.

He eventually filed a complaint with the Egyptian Foreign Ministry. He showed the officials our marriage certificate and the three children's birth certificates, which I had luckily left behind in Cairo. "My children are Egyptian citizens," he argued. "Egypt cannot just consent to them disappearing abroad. I have a right to know where my children are."

After giving up on making any headway, he returned to his job in Dubai. Then, one day, he received a call from the Foreign Ministry in Cairo. The official told him to set off immediately to Beijing. "After a long negotiation with Beijing, we have been notified that your children will be allowed to leave. So please arrange your flight and pick up your children immediately."

Of course, Mahmud didn't hesitate. "I dropped everything I was doing at my new job in Dubai and flew straight out here to you," he said.

I kissed him. "I thought you had forgotten about me a long time ago."

"You are the mother of my children. How could I forget you?"

"Regardless, thank you."

"I'm your husband. I did nothing more than my duty," he replied.

We slept well that night in the Egyptian ambassador's guest house, even though we were far from safe. The problem was that I had no passport and couldn't leave the country without one. So I desperately needed valid travel documents.

In concrete terms, I had to deal with the Chinese authorities again in Beijing. The police in Qarqan had given me a discharge certificate with which I had to report to the national state police. Mr. at-Taberi went with me since the ambassador thought it was too dangerous to leave me on my own.

As expected, the police did their best to place obstacles in my path. "We're sorry, but there's nothing we can do for you" were words I heard more than once.

"But I need a document to prove my identity."

"You should have thought about that before now. In any case, we cannot issue you a passport."

They sent me from agency to agency; I spoke with employees at five different offices. But they had the upper hand. As long as I had no document to prove my identity, the ambassador couldn't issue me a visa, and we couldn't leave for Egypt. But, on the other hand, we couldn't stay at the embassy forever. So they *had* to provide me with an identification card. There was no way around that.

After a lot of back and forth and considerable pressure from the ambassador, they declared themselves ready to supply me with at least a provisional document. According to the officials, this was a substitute for a regular identification card, on which my name, date of birth, birthplace, and affiliation with the Xinjiang province was printed. However, this card would only be valid for two months, so we had no time to lose.

That evening, Mahmud contacted his friend in Dubai and asked him to purchase tickets for us. We didn't have a computer with us, and Mahmud's phone, in which we had stuck a local SIM card, only had limited functionality in China. It didn't have global internet capabilities. Mahmud was also in a hurry to return because he had long used up his vacation days. Therefore, his friend booked us tickets for the next day on an EgyptAir flight.

In the wee hours of the following morning, we packed our few earthly belongings and took a taxi to the airport. I kept glancing nervously in the rearview mirror as we struggled through the traffic. Was anyone following us? I could hardly see anything in the crowded streets. Finally, after driving for almost an hour, we reached the airport. One look at the clock assured me we were early enough since we had calculated enough time to spare.

We got into the line for the security checkpoint, and after twenty minutes, we reached the counter. The border officer inspecting the travel papers for all the passengers eyed my temporary identification document. "What is this supposed to be? Do you want to leave with this?" he asked. "I've never seen something like this!"

"Yes, of course! I was assured that this is a full-fledged passport replacement." As proof, I pointed to the visa that the Egyptian Ambassador issued me on the same document.

However, this didn't convince the officer. "If the Egyptians want to recognize this document, that is their business. It has nothing to do with us."

"But this is an official document issued by an official agency."

"That doesn't mean you can travel on it, though," he countered.

By this point, the border guard had noticed that Xinjiang was noted on my identification document as my home province. That complicated the procedure. The guard asked me to step out of line so my family and I wouldn't hold up the other waiting passengers. He then waved to a colleague for support, who scanned my temporary ID and sent it somewhere.

"I can travel on this document," I reiterated. "They promised that I could. You can call the agency and verify that." In my mind, I added: And please hurry; otherwise, our plane will leave without us.

But the two officers didn't pay any attention to my comments; one of them was on the phone at this point. He said "Yes" and "I understand" several times, casting ongoing contemptuous looks at me as he did so. He then took me to a separate room, where I met other officers who were special unit members. They interrogated me extensively, claiming that my "case" hadn't yet been clarified to their satisfaction. I started to feel panicked; all this struck me as quite eerily familiar.

Mahmud never left my side. He, too, soon realized that the security officers were playing games with me once more. "You can see my wife has a visa," he declared. "Why won't you just let us leave?"

"Because we have to check out her story first," they insisted in a tone of voice that was probably meant to suggest that they were perfectly justified in behaving as they were.

"And how long will that take? We have to be at the gate in less than thirty minutes."

They just shrugged as if they couldn't have cared less. "You may leave whenever you like," they told Mahmud. "Your papers are in order, and the children may go with you. You still have enough time."

"We will not leave without my wife," he replied in frustration.

"That's your choice."

I exchanged a quick, meaningful glance with my husband. Like me, he knew exactly where all this was going; the officers had instructions to keep me in China. This was the only rationale for their so-called "examination." They were going to stall until the plane took off without me. On the other hand, they wanted to get rid of Mahmud and even offered him money to leave.

"Mihrigul is lost either way," one of the officers told him quite directly. "Why are you wasting your time with her? You could pocket a tidy sum of money and make a nice life if you'd take your children and go. With that money, you could get yourself another wife whenever you like. Just think about it."

Mahmud gazed at him, aghast, then slowly shook his head.

"You aren't all that bright," the officer declared. "Why are you picking this fight?"

At the end of the day, Mahmud and I returned to the Egyptian Embassy. We were exhausted by our stand-off with the security officers. The children also couldn't take it anymore and were in tears. This was a real low point. Above all, we had no idea what to do next.

The ambassador himself was at a loss. "You have valid papers and airline tickets," he said. "They *have* to let you go."

"Yes, theoretically, they do," Mahmud replied. "But if they keep running such extensive checks on us that we continue to miss our flights, I'll be bankrupt before long."

"You still need to try again."

We had to make four attempts. Mahmud's friend booked us on four other flights from Beijing to Cairo. We drove out to the airport four times, and three of those times, the planes took off without us. Even the fourth time, it looked as if we would fail again. After all, I presented a threat to them because a victim like me wasn't supposed to travel abroad and tell others about my persecution. That was why they kept offering Mahmud more and more money, but he never considered their offers for even one moment. His incorruptibility saved my life because I have no doubt whatsoever that if he had left me behind, they would have made short work of me.

Even as we stood at the check-in counter, I kept expecting them to fish me out of line again and send me back. I winced every time an announcement crackled over the speaker system, but Mahmud took my hand and spoke calming words. "Don't worry, Mihrigul," he said. "Allah is protecting us. Don't you see what a miracle it was that you were released from prison? Nothing is going to happen because His protective hand is over us."

And he was right. With each of us holding a child, we walked down the gangway and boarded the plane. Ten hours later, we found ourselves in another world. We had escaped.

CHAPTER 11

Homeless in Egypt

We reached Cairo at dawn. The April sun was shining warmly, suffusing the metropolis in a rosy glow, as we took the taxi into the city's center. Mahmud hadn't notified his parents of our arrival. After so many futile attempts to leave China, he wanted to be sure we would make it.

But now we were finally here and ringing the doorbell at the small apartment near the Nile Harbor, where my parents-in-law lived. My Egyptian mother-in-law was overjoyed when she opened the door and saw her son, her two grandchildren, and me standing on the threshold. She threw her arms around her son and me before snatching up the children and covering them with kisses. The two of them looked terrified and tried to hide behind my legs, but she showed no mercy. She exclaimed quite loudly, in sheer joy.

"Thank Allah! I can't believe you're here!" she kept saying as she struggled against waves of emotions, laughing, crying, proclaiming in joy, and back to crying at turns. "My poor, poor children, what all have you been through?"

"Just let them come inside, Mother!"

"I've waited so long for you! I prayed for you every day!"

The two children were now crying. They weren't just exhausted by the trip but didn't know what to make of this strange woman's odd behavior.

After she had mastered her first emotional outburst, my mother-in-law pushed us into the living room. We joined Mahmud's father on the floor cushions in there as she hurried into the kitchen to put the tea on. She then carried in all sorts of sweets and delicacies, which she had quickly pulled together from what she had on hand. She piled various pastries, dates, pistachios, oranges, and small green cucumbers in front of us. "Eat! You must be starving, so eat!" she kept urging us.

At that moment, I was very glad that Mahmud had never told his parents that my father had rejected them because he had wanted an Uyghur son-in-law. After the disastrous meetings between our families several years earlier – the only time I had met his parents before now – he had let them believe we had continued to be engaged. After the birth of our children and our trip back to my homeland, we planned to hold a large wedding celebration. That was why I was still Mahmud's bride to them, and during my absence, they had kept putting money aside for my bridal jewelry.

Mahmud's parents are both remarkably kind people. His mother, in particular, treated me so lovingly, as if I were her daughter. Noticing how tired I looked, she patted me on the head. "I'm so sorry about everything you've been through, dear child," she said, "but now it's over. Just rest and get your strength back." Then, she made a bed for us in Mahmud's childhood bedroom and ordered me to lie down there and sleep as long as I wanted. "You don't need to do anything, dear. I'll take care of everything," she promised. I hadn't experienced such motherly love since my childhood, and it brought me an unbelievable sense of peace. It enabled me to spend a lot of time during my first few days in Egypt simply relaxing, sleeping, and dozing.

My detention drained me physically and mentally, but I wasn't the only one. My children were also in a bad state and had to struggle with the repercussions of their internment. Things were especially bad for Moez. Due to his lung problems, he was supposed to sleep under a breathing mask, but this hadn't happened in the camp, so he was now constantly coughing and wheezing. During the nights, he frequently woke up because he couldn't get enough air.

At first, both children could barely keep down their food. As soon as they ate something, especially cooked meals, they vomited. That almost drove me to despair, considering how haggard they were. How could they gain weight if everything came back up again? My mother-in-law recognized the problem and started preparing special food for them on the second day. A few spoonfuls of rice or a small piece of bread was easier to digest than a complicated dish. "They were starving, so we have to get them used to food again," Mahmud's mother told me.

Nonetheless, the children's appetites were strong. Whenever they felt like they weren't being watched, they would slip into the kitchen to steal bread or other food. They didn't eat the food immediately but hid it in their beds. They would only enjoy their loot when they felt no one was watching them. If I walked in on them, they would jump up and run away with their food. They were scared that I would confiscate their pieces of bread or whatever they were eating at the moment. And regardless of how often I told them they could eat however much they wanted, Moez and Elena stubbornly maintained these precautions.

The two of them acted quite frightened around me; they must have been through terrible things while incarcerated. If I walked toward them from the front, they ducked away as if expecting to be beaten. It pained me that they didn't even trust their mother. They thought that I wanted to hurt them. "Why are you scared?" I asked them. "Who hurt you? I won't do anything to you!"

However, it was hard to communicate with them because Moez and Elena had lost much of their ability to speak in the camp. Before their arrest, they had babbled away in Uyghur, but now it was as if their vocabulary had evaporated. Most of the time, they just looked at me and said nothing. Occasionally, a few fragments of Chinese would tumble out of them. For example, Moez once asked me directly, "ni how ma" – "How are you doing?" in Chinese. Later, he told me that "Lalala" had beaten him. "Lalala" is a children's term for Han Chinese people.

It made me quite sad to realize how much my children had suffered, which was why I was so very sensitive during this time. My poor mother-in-law felt this, although she did everything possible to make my life as pleasant as possible. She could sense my sadness and often paid me compliments to console me. "You're so delicate and sweet, not as coarse and uncouth as Egyptian women," she declared once. "You are the daughter I never had."

Sometimes it was too much for me, at which point I would hiss at Mahmud that she needed to leave me alone. "What did she say?" his mother would ask.

"Nothing. She only said that she thinks your headscarf with the silver embroidery is very pretty."

"Oh, really?" And to brighten my day a little, she immediately knotted the scarf around my head. "It's yours now," she announced. "My gift to you!"

"No, I can't accept this," I replied. But when she insisted, I smiled bashfully and thanked her.

"She simply wants you to be alright. Just accept her affection," Mahmud said to me later. I took his advice to heart. I wouldn't have survived that dark time without him and his parents. My depression would have defeated me.

Unfortunately, Mahmud couldn't stay with us for long. He was still working for his old company in Dubai, which had granted him only one week of vacation. He had already been gone for four weeks, and his boss had sent him several nasty letters because he hadn't returned. So it was pressing that he returns.

"Just stay with my parents for a while and recuperate while I take care of things there," Mahmud said to me. We didn't have many other options since his income was critical, considering the high costs our family had incurred. Therefore, I encouraged him to return to Dubai only a few days after our arrival. "I'll come and get the three of you as soon as possible. Or I'll open another shop in Cairo so we can live together as a family," he promised me.

Mahmud's parents implored us to finally hold our wedding ceremony, which had been postponed for years. This would have ideally taken place before his departure, but there wasn't enough time for that. At their request, though, we went to a photographer's studio and had our portrait taken in festive garb as a bridal couple. This picture would normally be displayed in the room where the wedding guests would be greeted. But instead, his parents placed it in a prominent location on their living room bureau. I was delighted by this place of honor and enjoyed looking at the portrait. And for visitors, it proved we were a legitimate couple, even though the great celebration hadn't been held yet.

After Mahmud left, we pursued our normal day-to-day routine, which mainly revolved around the children and their health problems. We didn't hear from him right away, but this didn't cause me alarm. Mahmud had lots to catch up on after returning to work, and I assumed he hadn't contacted us.

However, once a week passed, I started to feel uneasy. It was particularly strange that he didn't respond to my WhatsApp messages. Before taking off, Mahmud had acquired an Egyptian SIM card for my phone so that we could stay in touch. And now he wasn't responding! Had something happened to him?

I eventually dialed the number of one of his friends, who also came from Egypt and worked in Dubai. Mahmud had left me his number in case of an emergency, and his friend immediately knew who I was. "Mihrigul," he said. "I've heard so much about you!"

"I can't seem to reach Mahmud anymore, and I'm getting worried," I told him.

"Yes, well… don't worry." Unfortunately, his voice didn't reassure me. "Mahmud can't respond at the moment because, uh… he's with the police."

"With the police?" I gasped for air. "What's he doing there? What going on with him?"

"Well… he was arrested when he returned to Dubai and is still in custody. His company is suing him for being gone for so long without permission. They're claiming that he used his employment contract to get a visa for Dubai…."

"But that's ridiculous!"

"Yes, but this is Dubai. The corporations here have a lot of power over their foreign employees."

I couldn't believe it. We were talking about Dubai, after all, not China. Did the same despotism overshadow everything there as well? Or did the Chinese somehow have their fingers in his arrest? It occurred to me that China does a lot of business in Dubai and presumably had some clout there. Maybe that was what was behind all this.

"But as I said, don't worry," the Egyptian man on the other end of the line tried to reassure me. "I'm sure he'll be released quite soon. He hasn't done anything wrong, after all."

I hadn't done anything wrong, either, and had still landed in prison, I thought. Was this going to be Mahmud's fate as well? I started to cry.

"Come on, don't cry! You'll see, everything's going to be just fine. At any rate, I'll keep you informed."

"Thank you. That would be nice of you."

After I hung up, I considered whether or not to tell my in-laws about this latest development. However, I felt it was my fault that Mahmud was in trouble, so I kept the information to myself for the time being.

Shortly after that, Mahmud called. He was in his friend's apartment. "Everything's just fine, Mihrigul," he said, emphatically optimistic. He told me that the head of the company for which he was working had been so angry about his absence that he had filed a complaint with the authorities while he was in China. That was why the police picked him up as soon as he landed. So now he was out of work and locked in a legal battle with his former employer.

I considered his news for a moment. That wasn't good, but it meant Mahmud no longer had ties to Dubai. So he could return to Cairo and attempt to start something new with me by his side. "When are you coming back?" I asked him.

"That won't be so easy."

"Why not?"

"The police took away my passport."

"For what reason?"

"As long as the lawsuit against me is still open, I'm not allowed to leave the country." I gulped. "I'm so sorry."

Could this really be happening? I wondered. Would Allah play such a macabre joke on us? After all that we'd been through? Now that I needed Mahmud more than anyone else, He couldn't separate us again!

But that was precisely our situation. Without his passport, Mahmud was stuck in Dubai indefinitely. On the other hand, I was in Cairo, where I possessed no valid travel documents either.

I now faced having to tell his parents the truth, for better or worse. "Until the courts have settled the matter, Mahmud isn't allowed to leave the country," I told my father-in-law, for whom it was a catastrophe that his son couldn't earn an income to support the two children and me. He and his wife had only his modest pension to live on. "His apartment was also seized."

"We have to be patient. Allah won't abandon us," the devout man declared. Regardless, I could tell that he was feeling a little sick. We both wondered if everything was just and above board. Or was I the intended target of this harassment? After all, we were dealing with a powerful opponent.

"We need to clarify your residency status as quickly as possible and obtain an ID card for you," my father-in-law declared. "That way, they won't...." He bit his lip, but I knew what he'd been about to say.

"That way, they won't deport me to China," I finished the sentence for him with a shudder. This danger was quite real.

So I went to the registry office and showed the administrative official my entry document with its Chinese characters and my marriage license, which Mahmud had fortunately left at his parent's apartment. "I would like to apply for an ID," I told the older gentleman with the meticulously parted hair, who eyed me first before turning to my documents.

"But you are a foreigner!"

"Yes, but I'm married to an Egyptian." I pointed at the marriage license, which was slightly crumpled and yellowed by this point, but still legible.

"And where is your husband?"

"He is abroad."

"But he needs to be here!"

"He can't come. Isn't the marriage license enough?"

"Your husband has to confirm your identity.'"

I thought about this. "What about his father? Couldn't he vouch for him?"

The official grumbled something. "Whatever," he finally said. "Come back with your father-in-law next time. And bring a notarized translation of your temporary passport as well, please."

After this first sounding out, I felt cautiously optimistic. For my next appointment with the officials, I brought along my father-in-law and produced the requested and notarized translation of my provisional travel documents, including the attached visa.

"Hmm," the official said, bending over my papers. "So you're from Xinjiang. Isn't it quite difficult to get out of there?" He furrowed his brow. "This document is also only good for two months. That period's almost up."

I felt that this conversation was taking a turn for the worse. "Yes, I know," I told the official. "You are exactly right. It is quite hard to get out of Xinjiang at the moment, which is why I'm so glad to be here."

"But if your identification papers lapse, your visa will expire, too."

"I don't think so."

"I'll need to verify this," the official declared. "Either way, I'm amazed they let you enter the country on this."

These words were the prelude to intensive research by the Egyptian authorities. Just one week later, I received a call from the border police. The officer on the other end of the line asked me several questions about the reasons for my departure. "How were you able to leave the country from the Xinjiang province?" she wanted to know. "And why don't you have a normal Chinese passport? Who issued you this temporary document?"

The responses I supplied apparently made her more curious because I received another call about a week later. This time it was from someone with a different unit that was focused on human trafficking.

"I'm here legally!" I insisted to the officer on the phone.

"But your papers aren't in order."

How could you do this to me, I thought. "We were in a hurry to leave the country. If you don't believe me, ask your ambassador in China."

"We will be pursuing whatever lines of inquiry are necessary," the man affirmed. "I also have to ask you to meet with us in person. Would some time next week work for you? And you should plan on being here for a while since this matter seems fairly complicated."

I felt hot and cold. The summons from the police reminded me vividly of my experiences in Qarqan. I immediately started to have flashbacks to the numerous interrogations I'd been through there. What if the Chinese pressured the Egyptians to send me back? There was a chance that I couldn't leave the Cairo police station as a free woman – and I might unexpectedly find myself back in a cell in Qarqan. That was why everything inside of me screamed, "No! Never again! Don't go to the police!"

So I skipped the appointment. Instead, I set up a new profile on Facebook and began to search there for Uyghurs living abroad, like me. Perhaps some of them might have had experience with situations like mine and could help me. That was how I stumbled across all sorts of activists. I also found a journalist who had interviewed various Uyghurs for Radio Free Asia. She painted a bleak picture of the situation in Xinjiang. This woman would at least understand what I was going through, and maybe she would have some advice for me. So I sent her a message via the Messenger app.

I waited anxiously for her response, but nothing happened. Maybe she wasn't on Facebook much, wasn't interested in replying, or had a policy of not responding to such messages. Since I had included my Egyptian phone number, there was also a chance that she would call me. Ten days later, I did receive a call from an unknown number.

"Hello?" I said.

"Mihrigul!" I heard my father's voice. I felt like I'd been struck by lightning; this was one thing I never thought would happen. I was thrilled to hear from him, but I was also shocked. How had he gotten my Egyptian number?

"Papa!" I finally managed to say.

He got straight to the point. "Mihrigul, we know where you are," he said somberly. "What are you doing in Egypt? China is your homeland…."

That was when I knew he wasn't alone. A Chinese officer had to sit beside him, forcing him to have this conversation.

"Are you in or out?" I asked him.

"What are you talking about?"

"You know what I mean."

"Nothing has happened to us. Nobody did anything to you," he chattered away. "So stop your shenanigans. Come back! Or do you want to ruin your entire family? Do you know how many of us are now in trouble because of you?"

After that, the connection died, but that last question struck home. Yes, I wondered: What was I doing here anyway? Weren't my escapades slowly reaching their end? I had dragged my entire family into the abyss. Maybe I should go back to China and face the authorities. At least, it would help protect my parents from any further harm.

I realized that the short conversation with my father had served its purpose as far as the Chinese authorities were concerned. It left me feeling very confused and doubtful as to whether I had done the right thing. The long arm of manipulation had even reached me thousands of miles away from the Chinese prison cells. I had to be on my guard to keep from falling into the clutches of my opponents. I couldn't lower my guard now!

I opened Facebook Messenger again and saw that the journalist had finally written back. "Hey, Mihrigul, let's talk! I would like to hear your story," she wrote.

We arranged to chat the following day. In a long phone call, I told her about my suffering in the Xinjiang camps and my current difficulties in Egypt. "I think the Chinese are after me again," I told her.

"That's no surprise," she said. "The information you have is very explosive. Nobody is supposed to know about the torture going on in these camps. It's a state secret."

Even as she said the words, I knew that the phrase "state secret" was no exaggeration. I did have information the Chinese government would want to keep secret at all costs. No one in the world was supposed to know what the Chinese were doing to us Uyghurs in our homeland. But I, Mihrigul Tursun, was in a position to report on it. For the first time, I sensed the power that this gave me. I didn't have only the opportunity but also the obligation to tell the world about the heinous crimes against my people. The people trapped in the overcrowded prison cells demanded nothing less than this. I had escaped, but I couldn't just forget about the countless prisoners in my homeland. And so I made a decision.

"I want you to publish everything," I told the journalist, "everything I've told you."

"I'd love to do that," she said. "But I don't think you'll be safe in Egypt after that."

"I'm not now as it is. You know where I am."

I asked her to record my voice, at least, in case something happened to me, or I was deported. My eyewitness account would be preserved that way. I owed this to my fellow sufferers in the cells and my deceased son. "If I disappear suddenly, you can publish this," I told her.

After that, I didn't hear from her for a while. However, I kept getting calls from the police, demanding I finally show up for questioning. "It is important that you come in for this. We are now in contact with the Chinese authorities," they said. I made several appointments but didn't keep any of them. This couldn't go on much longer. I then received another call from a number I didn't recognize. I considered whether I should answer it; generally, calls like this didn't bode well. But I answered it anyway.

"Am I speaking with Mihrigul Tursun?" a woman asked in Arabic, though with an accent.

"Yes, who is this?" I asked hesitantly.

"This is Jennifer from the American Embassy." She told me she had gotten my number from the journalist and asked if we could meet in person. I understood she didn't want to say anything else on the phone. "This afternoon at four o'clock at the McDonald's near the harbor?" That was just two streets away from me. She obviously knew where I was living. Be careful, Mihrigul, my inner voice warned me. It might be a trap. Or an opportunity.

"Yes, alright," I said.

That afternoon, I left the children with my mother-in-law and set off to the specified McDonald's. I didn't have far to walk. Jennifer told me she would be sitting outside wearing a blue jacket. I recognized her instantly with her light blonde hair and carefully styled pageboy cut. She was sitting at the table with two other women.

"Hi, I'm Jennifer," she said in greeting as she held out her hand. "Thank you for coming."

She had already ordered soft drinks for all of us and introduced me to the other two women at the table. One of them was another American, a colleague from the U.S. Embassy. The other woman was Egyptian and had been hired by the others as an interpreter. Jennifer, who was the leader of the group, came straight to the point. "We heard that you're from Xinjiang and went through some terrible things there," she said.

I nodded, involuntarily glancing around me. Was there a camera somewhere watching us or someone taking pictures of us? After my interrogations in Qarqan, where they had confronted me over and over again with pictures from Egypt, I couldn't stop thinking about the fact that China had eyes and ears everywhere. I experienced that firsthand, so I was incredibly reticent at the start of our conversation. In my subconscious, I automatically reckoned that everything I was saying was being recorded and would be used against me later. So I just replied with "yes" and "no."

"Don't you feel safe with us?" Jennifer asked. "Are you uncomfortable talking to us?"

"I do!" I declared. "It's just that... Could we possibly go for a walk?"

She now glanced around a little suspiciously as well. "Yes, of course," she said. "We should've been doing that all along."

And so we walked along the harbor. Jennifer explained to me that her country's government was concerned about the plight of the Uyghurs. However, at the moment, it wasn't proving easy to find out about the situation there, which was why they had contacted me. "Our members of Congress are trying to form their own opinions, so they can decide how the US should handle China in the future," she explained. "And that is why it is critical for them to know firsthand how the Uyghurs are being treated."

This astonished me. I couldn't quite understand why a foreign country would be concerned about our situation and what China was doing to us. But, nonetheless, I was glad that somebody somewhere cared about our fate.

"Would you like to testify as a witness before the U.S. Congress?" Jennifer asked me.

I didn't know precisely what "the Congress" was. It sounded like a tribunal, but honestly, this wasn't a major factor for me. It was now my mission to tell the world about the atrocities committed by the Chinese against my people. Their crimes against me, my children, and all the other Uyghurs had to be made public. I would have talked to anyone willing to listen. "Absolutely," I said.

"The United States will grant you asylum in return. This way, you won't have to worry about any problems caused by testifying," Jennifer said.

"Really? Does that mean I can stay in America afterward?"

"Yes, you may."

I was speechless. Had Allah once more heard my desperate prayers? "Thank you," I whispered.

"It would be best if you didn't leave your apartment until then," she advised me. "Pack up your things and wait for my call."

Jennifer pulled up at my door in an embassy vehicle three days later.

CHAPTER 12

My New Life, in the Shadows of the Old One

I had nothing to wear. Frowning, Jennifer studied the three outfits hanging in the closet of my basement apartment in Washington. The dark blouses and robes I'd wrapped myself in during the Egyptian summer didn't seem suitable to her, so she decided to take me shopping. "You can't run around in all black and trying to hide," she declared. "We need something business-like for you."

Jennifer, who had picked up my children and me from my in-laws' apartment in Cairo and loaded us into business class on an American Airlines flight to Washington, was my most important contact in our new home. As a U.S. State Department staff member, she was specially assigned in November 2018 to organize my appearance before Congress and my relocation to the United States. My parents-in-law had sympathetically agreed to this when I presented them with this opportunity. "It is the right thing for you to do," my father-in-law strongly encouraged me before our departure.

We drove together to a shopping mall, where Jennifer searched for an understated two-piece outfit for me. We also bought a pair of pumps to go along with it. When I saw myself in the mirror, I felt like an attorney in an American TV series, but Jennifer thought it was the right look. "Do you want something to wear on your head?" she asked. I nodded. And so we continued to a different shop and purchased a pretty silk scarf in variegated blue tones. It was supposed to emphasize my Muslim identity. When Jennifer finally saw my new look, she was quite satisfied. "You look nice!" she declared. "Nothing will go wrong the day after tomorrow."

My grand appearance was two days later. We had worked on my statement to Congress for almost two months by then. With the help of an interpreter, Jennifer had me tell her every detail of my stay in the prison camps so that she could verify the facts. She and her co-workers often had follow-up questions for me. They then compiled all the reports into a single compact witness statement for me.

I read through and doublechecked this text repeatedly – both the English and the Uyghur versions – as I sat in Jennifer's office with my children. I had described to her the methods of torture the guards had used on me during their interrogations. I had even sketched the angles at which the cameras in the cells had been mounted. The location of the cuts on my children's necks had also been noted in my file. "It is important that every detail is correct," Jennifer reminded me, inquiring several times if the names of places and individuals in the report were also accurate. I reassured her they were. Seeing everything documented on paper in black and white felt strange, but it also felt good. I finally had everything that had happened to me and that I knew about the Chinese internment system written down. Of course, I felt fairly safe in the United States, but I thought if something still happened to me, at least there was this document.

As we were driving back home in a taxi after that appointment, I suddenly noticed two bright headlights in the driver's rearview mirror. I tensed up. Could this just be coincidental? Was this just some driver who wanted to tailgate us, or was someone following us? I verified that my children, who were sitting in the backseat with me, were seat-belted. "Could you drive faster?" I asked the driver.

"No problem, ma'am," replied the driver, an Indian man in a turban, as he pressed the gas pedal. Our car raced along the highway at over one hundred miles an hour. However, the vehicle following us matched our speed.

My heart was pounding; the other car refused to be shaken off. The taxi driver also noticed that something was wrong. He picked up even more speed, but that didn't change anything. The other vehicle even gained on us a little before changing lanes. Was it going to pass us? No, the car closed in on us from the side. It got so close that our side mirror snapped off.

The taxi driver cursed. "You asshole! I'll report you!" he bellowed. "Ma'am, he's trying to cut us off. I think he wants us to stop...."

"Please, for the love of God, don't do that!" I begged him. My children were sobbing in fright. The vehicle was already passing us and trying to get in front of the taxi; he wanted to cut us off. I had the presence of mind to pull out my phone and take a picture of the other car's license plate. It was a Mexican tag. In the meantime, the taxi driver managed to make a hard right onto a side street, effectively ditching our pursuer.

"Oh, my God," I said, exhaling deeply. "Thank you. You handled that well."

"Do you know that guy?" he asked.

"No," I replied truthfully. The driver had looked Latino. "Never seen him before."

We sped through the streets for a while longer until we were sure that we really had left that guy behind us—the driver then stopped at a police station and filed a report against the unknown driver.

"Do you have any suspicions about who might have done this?" the USCP officer filling out the paperwork asked me. "Is there anyone out there who might wish you harm?" I almost laughed out loud in light of how grotesque this question sounded. Yes, the government of the second most powerful nation in the world, I thought.

I showed the officer the photo I had taken so that he could run a check on the license plate number. And he was successful at identifying the owner of the car. It belonged to an undocumented Mexican immigrant who was scheduled for deportation. I am convinced that he had been hired as a contract killer.

That night, I slept quite poorly. I was sharing a bed with Elena and Moez, and we held each other's hands. We often did that to assure ourselves that we weren't alone. It calmed the children to feel close to me. As I listened to their even breathing, I tried to gather strength for my big day. But every time I dozed off, I jolted awake, convinced I had heard noises. Was someone creeping around our building? Or was someone trying to break into our apartment? I wasn't sure if my enemies knew where I lived, but they knew which taxi I'd taken.

I woke up the next morning feeling rather strung out. I padded over to the kitchenette and brewed a strong cup of tea to get myself going. When I felt more steady, I woke up Elena and Moez and dressed them in their nicest clothes. As the children ate their cornflakes, I put on the outfit that Jennifer had gotten for me. And then it was time. The car sent over for us by the State Department was already pulling up at the door. It drove the children and me to the center of Washington, to the Capitol.

It was a great moment for me as we stepped inside the venerable, white stone building with its powerful dome, which I had only ever seen on television. One of Jennifer's co-workers took us to a room where the children could play while I was being made up for my appearance. By this point, my excitement and nervousness were rising. Before everything started, I ensured Moez and Elena were doing alright. "Where are you going, Mama?" they asked.

"I'll be right back. I need to go get us some sweets," I lied. I left them with the babysitter because the politicians were waiting for me.

The space in which the hearing took place was huge and paneled in dark wood. I was startled to see how many people were sitting there, about 300 politicians and members of the press. Way up at the front stood a stage on which chairs had been arranged in a semicircle. I took my seat there next to an interpreter. All the journalists pointed their microphones and cameras at me, and the chatter in the room died away. I blinked sheepishly as the spotlights blinded me.

"Thank you very much for being with us today, Mihrigul Tursun," a politician said in greetings. I had no idea who he was.

I nodded and thanked him for the invitation. As my voice echoed over the loudspeaker into the room, it sounded scratchy. I was also uncertain whether the people gathered there could understand my English. And yet I kept in mind that the U.S. government would be asking me questions, and it was my job to answer them accordingly. Fortunately, I didn't have to speak at first, only listen. The interpreter read my witness statement for me.

My face grew numb as I listened to her – more accurately, my – report. I felt strangely detached from what was going on around me. Was I actually the person to whom all of these atrocities had happened? I felt increasingly like a spectator watching a film or a theater performance. But then the interpreter reached the spot where I described my son's death in the Ürümqi hospital. I could suddenly feel his swaddled body in my arms. Tears welled in my eyes, and I gazed into the faces of the members of Congress and saw their horror as well.

After reading my testimony, the politician who had spoken to me previously said: "We have listened to your story, and your account sits here in front of us, but we would like to hear more from you personally. Would it be alright if we asked you some questions?"

I nodded. Of course, that was what I had planned to do all along. But when the first questions began, I could feel my anxiety suddenly spike. I felt unwell because the questions reminded me of my interrogations in China. I subconsciously expected to be punished, for them to inflict pain on me. What would happen if I didn't know the answer to one of their questions? I kept wondering. And then everything in my mind went dark, and I couldn't answer anything.

"Is everything alright, Ms. Tursun?" the politician asked. "Should we perhaps take a break?"

"No," I replied, as I tried to focus on the fact that I wasn't in a Chinese interrogation room here. These people didn't wish to harm me; they wouldn't torture me or lock me in a cell. They were only interested in what I had suffered through, and they might even help me make my powerful enemies pay for what they had done to me. "I'm just fine. We can continue," I said resolutely.

The politicians asked me a lot of questions. I answered them sometimes in Uyghur and sometimes in English. The hearing lasted for a total of two hours. After that, I felt exhausted but also content that I had been able to provide these influential people with insights into the unbelievable crimes that were being perpetrated against my fellow Uyghurs.

Nonetheless, I cannot say I was happy once this ended. There will be no more happiness in my life. The Chinese government tortured me too much for that. They robbed me of the joys of motherhood, of the experience of holding my babies to my breast and being there for them. I will never have that opportunity again, nor will I ever be as joyful and carefree as I was before my incarceration. Even the powerful American politicians couldn't give this back to me any more than they could bring back my deceased son or the family I'd been forced to leave behind. This was why my desire for revenge ended in a void. Regardless of what I might still do with my life, it can never compensate for the painful and tragic losses I was forced to endure. I will never be able to make my tormenters pay enough. I grasped all this in that one moment.

Later, I spoke to a psychologist about all of this. I told him that there was nothing I longed for more than to undo that horrible time in Xinjiang or to at least be able to forget about it. "Please give me a pill to wipe everything out of my mind," I begged him, "so I can once again live freely." But unfortunately, there is no medicine for that. I'm doomed to carry the memories of the torture I experienced with me for the rest of my days.

Sadly, it is the same for my children. After the hearing, I picked them up, bringing the sweets I had promised. I had gotten gummy bears and bars of chocolate for them out of a vending machine. "Were you good while I was gone?" I asked, glancing over at the babysitter. My children can sometimes be stressful, especially if they don't know someone. Time and again, I've observed behaviors that reveal that they are still burdened by their time in captivity. They escaped the camp, of course, but the anguish they experienced is still embedded in their bodies and minds.

The fact that they feel uncomfortable around strangers – and even hide from them sometimes – is a symptom of my children's awful experiences in the camp. They are quite fearful, and both are scared of animals, especially dogs. If we run into these four-legged creatures at the park, my children take flight because the dogs remind them of the night of my last arrest. At that time, the police officers had surrounded our bed with large, furiously barking dogs. This experience traumatized my children, and even to this day, it seems to have seeped into their bones.

At night, Moez always makes sure that I am there. He prefers it when I go to sleep next to him, holding his hand. If I don't do that, he keeps coming into the living room to ensure I am still there. He is deathly terrified of losing me again.

Occasionally my son surprises me with bouts of aggression, which at first glance don't seem to fit his otherwise gentle nature. For example, when we were on the airplane, he spotted a man and a woman from Korea sitting behind us. Their eyes resembled those of the Han Chinese, and apparently, the sight of this triggered in him memories of his time in the camp. Anyway, he suddenly got incredibly upset and started to loudly explain that he would beat up the two "ni how." He used the Chinese equivalent of "How are you" as a synonym for "Chinese people." As he said this, he was already jumping out of his seat to carry out his announcement, and I could barely grab hold of him. "You can't just run off and hit strangers, Moez," I warned him. "That's not acceptable." He sobbed in rage.

Another time, not so long ago, we were out on the sidewalk, watching a demonstration against the new trade sanctions that China had authorized against the United States. I can't recall what products were involved, but the protesters were upset about the high tariffs Beijing would soon impose on their export goods. The demonstrators held signs in the air and shouted, "China, go home." Moez heard this, and it pleased him. Since then, my son hasn't stopped uttering this slogan.

When I picked Moez up from daycare the following day, his teacher took me aside. "This has to stop," she told me. "Your son isn't allowed to indoctrinate the other children politically."

At first, I had no idea what she was talking about. "Did Moez do something wrong?" I asked her point-blank.

"He told the other children they had to line up and repeat political slogans."

"What kind of slogans?"

"China, go home." She shook her head disapprovingly, and I blushed in embarrassment. However, inside I was on the verge of tears as I wondered what experiences Moez had been processing here. Had he also been forced to line up inside the camp and shout slogans as I had? Had the Chinese carried out their brainwashing agenda against children as well?

Regarding our health, all three of us still struggle with the repercussions of our internment. My daughter has eye problems and must wear glasses because she is half-blind. Unfortunately, the surgery to realign her eyes failed. And my son still struggles to get enough air in his lungs. He sleeps every night under an oxygen mask and has had several operations.

According to the doctors, he developed an infection and subsequently a cyst due to the cut made in the side of his throat that I had discovered when the children were returned to me in Ürümqi. This growth cuts off his air passages. His nose was damaged by the tube they had inserted there. As a result of that prolonged air deprivation, his testicles are also undersized. In addition, he cannot hold much urine; I had to put him in diapers for a long time because he would wet the bed at night.

As for me, shortly after we arrived in the United States, I started to take antidepressants at the recommendation of a psychiatrist. As a result of all the terrible things I'd been through, I suffered from PTSD, which triggered my depression. The doctors' determination that I am now infertile troubled me more than anything. I would have loved to have more children with Mahmud, but I assume this is because of the medication they forced me to take in the camp. Furthermore, I have a strange skin rash that nobody can explain.

My biggest problem, though, is my right ear. Because of the beating I received, the vein behind my ear ruptured and bleeds continuously. My ear then fills with pus and aches. It has to be cleaned out once a week to prevent an infection from spreading to my brain. I need to have surgery on my head, but I don't have health insurance that could cover that procedure.

Over the past three years, my life in the United States hasn't been particularly stable. My children and I were granted full asylum due to my willingness to testify in front of Congress. In December 2018, I also received a human rights prize, the Citizen Power Award, for my testimony. I am very happy that we can live in the United States and that I received an award for telling my story. Nonetheless, our early days here were anything but easy. I was forced to move five times because of repeated attempts to intimidate me. It was terrifying to realize that China's long arm could reach as far as Washington, D.C.

Once, for example, I was at a mall to pick up a few things for the children. As the three of us went from one clothing store to another, I noticed two Chinese people following us everywhere. I initially thought that maybe they were just there by coincidence. You already see ghosts; I scolded myself. But when I entered a fast food restaurant to get the children some fries, they followed us there and sat down at a table very close to ours. And then they proceeded to take pictures of us there.

I started to panic. Moez and Elena could also sense something was wrong, and they began to squirm restlessly in their seats. What should I do? There was no way I would go home now and show them where we were living. I eventually called the FBI from our table and explained to the officers there that these two individuals were following me. They showed up a short time later. When they checked the personal IDs of my two pursuers, it turned out that they were staff members from the Chinese Embassy in Washington.

However, even though I prevented them from following me home on that occasion, they could still discover my address. Then, one night, I received a horrible fright when someone knocked loudly on our door. Of course, that couldn't mean anything good. My children, who had also awakened, were scared by the noise. They were paralyzed in the bed and asked me who was at the door. "I don't know," I whispered, trying not to show my fear too clearly. "I'll go see."

"No!" Moez shouted. He and Elena clutched my hands tightly and tried to keep me from going. I preferred to stay in bed with them, but the knocking wouldn't stop. I wanted to look through my peephole and see who was terrorizing us.

"I won't open the door," I promised my children.

On silent soles, I padded through the darkness to the apartment door and peered through the hole. However, the person on the other side must have noticed me approaching because he covered the hole with his finger. I held my breath; he knew I was standing on the other side. I stood motionlessly at that spot for a while but then slipped back to bed.

I cuddled with my children there. "Don't be scared," I said in an attempt to soothe them, although I felt anything but calm. The knocking had stopped by then, but I wondered if the man was still standing there.

Suddenly, there was a loud crashing sound quite close to us. My children screamed. A brick had been lobbed through our bedroom window, shattering the pane. The cold night air rushed inside as I clutched my children in terror. It was only after my paralysis thawed that I was able to dial 911. It took the police only two minutes to reach us.

"You need to move, ma'am," advised the FBI officer investigating this incident. "You aren't safe here." We moved to our new place, the second of our five homes, three days later.

In our new apartment, I met with FBI officers to increase the security of our home. They installed cameras at our front door and windows, which would transmit footage to a screen in my bedroom. This way, I would always be able to see what was happening outside – and in case of an emergency, I could hit an alarm button. At least, that was the theory.

However, shortly after my relocation, my pursuers told me they also had this address. They started by carving a cross in my front door.

Then they got more direct; they pushed a folded piece of paper through the newspaper slot. "We know everything about you: what you eat, where you live, where your children are in daycare." I read this note written in Chinese characters. "It would be best for you to keep your mouth shut from now on."

Speechless, I lowered the paper. How could this have happened? How did they get this into my apartment when the outside door area was under camera surveillance?

I showed the paper to an officer, who took it to check for fingerprints. He also went through the camera footage but could not identify the visitor who had left the note for me. All we could see was his gloved hands pushing the paper through the slot.

"The guy took advantage of the one blind spot," the officer said with a mixture of disgust and professional respect. "This was a true professional at work."

Even today, I haven't been able to shake off my pursuers from my old homeland. I have almost gotten used to the fact that they always find me eventually. A Chinese woman recently moved into my neighborhood, a patriot who only patronizes Chinese businesses. Is it just a coincidence that she is now my neighbor? Is she spying on me? I don't know, but I no longer let myself feel intimidated. I have to live with my fear. As for myself, I have decided that no one will ever silence me again.

Many Uyghurs who live in Washington feel differently. They fear China's long shadow and behave with the corresponding caution. That is why they give me a wide berth. They know that I testified before Congress and am, thus, on China's hit list. Therefore, whenever there is an event about the Uyghurs, and the situation in our homeland is supposed to be discussed with frankness, I am always supposed to come and get on the stage to speak. However, they prefer not to invite me to private celebrations like weddings. They also never want to take a photo with me since these might land on Facebook or Instagram. And if I appear in a picture next to them, they black out my face so that no Chinese censor will recognize me, the whistle-blower.

They justify these precautions by referring to their families in Xinjiang. "We can't jeopardize those left behind," they say. It cuts me deeply because I, too, have family back there. Their comments reveal that these other Uyghurs are frightened that China will take revenge on them. They haven't freed themselves on the inside yet. The brainwashing is still intact, and none are willing to take a brave stand.

It takes tremendous inner strength to do that. I often lack this strength, too, but then I must remember that I am obligated to speak the truth, even if I have to pay a high price. Who else is going to do it? The ones left behind definitely can't.

My parents can't speak up, either. So I have to assume the worse for them. I assume that they are being tortured in a detention camp. I only hear from them when the Chinese government wants to use them to pressure me. They called me twice in Egypt and begged me to return to prevent more of our relatives from being arrested. After my departure, my uncle, who had worked in Qarqan as a police officer and always protected me the best he could within his job, was sentenced to twelve years in prison. "Consider your relatives!" my father implored when I heard from him the last time. "Come back. We'll protect you!" But I didn't believe a word he said because it wasn't my Papa that I was speaking to. It was a tormented, terrified man being controlled by someone else.

Since starting my life in the United States, we haven't been in direct contact. It is better that way. However, I follow the Chinese government's online propaganda to discredit my story. They have made several videos in which my parents can be seen, having been forced by our torturers to bear witness against me.

In the last video, released in April 2021, my father said, "Mihrigul was never in a camp. She always lived in our home, and she was fine there. She excelled academically."

It hurt so much for me to hear something like this, but I don't hold it against him. Nobody living in China would run the risk of saying anything else. What bothers me is the thought that my relatives are being terrorized and threatened because I had the courage to speak the truth. I feel so bad about my family. At the same time, I am deeply convinced that I need to do what I'm doing. After all, the Chinese government is trying to liquidate an entire ethnic group.

Over a million people have shared my fate. Even as I write these lines, many are still in concentration camps, where they are being tortured and mistreated with incredible cruelty. Even if these people are released from the camps, they will never be the same again, as is the case for my family and me.

That is the goal, after all. By completely dehumanizing us through total surveillance and brainwashing, China wants to rob prisoners of their individual and cultural identity permanently. How can I do anything but scream to the world about the crime I was forced to experience in my own body? It is time for the rest of the world to wake up and do something about this.

In light of the loss of my family, it comforts me greatly that at least my husband and his parents continue to support and stand with me steadfastly. We speak on the phone practically every day. Recently, during a video chat, my mother-in-law pulled out a jewelry box and nestled inside were twelve gold bracelets. "I bought these for you," she announced proudly. "This is your wedding jewelry."

"What in the world were you thinking?" I scolded her.

The two of them always try to send me money, although they live on very limited means as a retired teacher and a retired pilot. My mother-in-law, who is already 87, often says she feels obligated to me. "I owe you this," she claims. "I couldn't support you when your children were small. I need to make up for that now."

"But I'm doing fine. I have a job, don't I?" I exclaimed in an attempt to get her to stop. I worked for some time at a pizzeria, but I couldn't earn much from that job, which later fell victim to the Covid pandemic. In actuality, I really could use their financial gifts.

Mahmud has been stuck in Dubai for three years and is still waiting for permission to leave the country. We very much hope that his situation will soon be resolved. It would be wonderful for us to be back together again, finally. I am tired of being alone, and the children long for nothing more than to see their father.

We sometimes look at photos from earlier, ones of Mahmud and me from ten years ago when we were getting to know each other in Cairo. I can hardly believe how young and carefree we both look when I see these pictures. Far too much has happened since then. Once, when the children were looking at the photos, they noticed one of me and my three babies, which had been taken shortly after they were born.

"But there are three babies here!" Elena immediately declared.

"Yes, here are the two of you. And the third baby is your brother, Mohammed."

"Where is he now?"

"He's with your Papa," I lied. This just tumbled out of me. Despite how much time has passed, I still cannot admit that my firstborn died in China.

"Will he come when Papa joins us?" Elena asked.

"Yes, definitely."

At some point, I will have to tell my daughter the truth, just not today. She is still too small to comprehend the horrendous truth.

Nonetheless, the world will learn from my mouth about the inconceivable crimes that are being committed against the Uyghurs. It is my mission. I survived to be able to bear this witness. Nobody should be able to later claim that they knew nothing about it.

ACKNOWLEDGMENTS

Numerous people are involved in the creation of a book, which is why we authors would like to thank the most significant ones on behalf of all of them.

The Uyghur human rights activist, Mihriban Mehmet, brought the two of us together. She stood by us as an interpreter, exhibiting great patience and cultural sensitivity during our long interview sessions.

Our editors at Heyne Verlag, Sophie Boysen, and Sara Ginolas, believed strongly in this project from the very beginning, as did our American publisher, Tracy C. Ertl.

The journalist Daniel Goffart accepted the task of critically reviewing our first draft.

Rachel Hildebrandt Reynolds handled the translation of the German manuscript into English.

The Uyghur journalist Gulchahra Hoja helped me escape from Egypt to the United States by notifying the U.S. government about my situation.

Congressmen Marco Rubio and Chris Smith also assisted me, as did the U.S. Embassy in Cairo.

Our agent Christine Proske came up with the idea for this book. She remains the driving force behind this project.

Last but not least, we wish to thank all of our readers for accompanying us on this journey through my difficult past and in telling my story so that the world will be informed about the terror being spread by the Chinese government. Nobody should ever be able to say that they knew nothing about this!

Thank you all from the bottom of our hearts,
 Mihrigul Tursun and Andrea Hoffmann